CHRISTINA AGUILERA

CHRISTINA AGUILERA

A Biography

Mary Anne Donovan

GREENWOOD BIOGRAPHIES

GREENWOOD

AN IMPRINT OF ABC-CLIO, LLC
Santa Barbara, California • Denver, Colorado • Oxford, England

Copyright 2010 by ABC-CLIO, LLC

All rights reserved. No part of this publication may be reproduced, stored in a retrieval system, or transmitted, in any form or by any means, electronic, mechanical, photocopying, recording, or otherwise, except for the inclusion of brief quotations in a review, without prior permission in writing from the publisher.

Library of Congress Cataloging-in-Publication Data

Donovan, Mary Anne.
   Christina Aguilera : a biography / Mary Anne Donovan.
      p. cm. — (Greenwood biographies)
   Includes bibliographical references and index.
   ISBN 978-0-313-38318-2 (alk. paper) — ISBN 978-0-313-38320-5
(ebook) 1. Aguilera, Christina, 1980– 2. Singers—United States—
Biography. I. Title.
   ML420.A337D66   2010
   782.42164092—dc22
   [B]   2010021178

ISBN: 978-0-313-38318-2
EISBN: 978-0-313-38320-5

14 13 12 11 10   1 2 3 4 5

This book is also available on the World Wide Web as an eBook.
Visit www.abc-clio.com for details.

Greenwood
An Imprint of ABC-CLIO, LLC

ABC-CLIO, LLC
130 Cremona Drive, P.O. Box 1911
Santa Barbara, California 93116-1911

This book is printed on acid-free paper ∞

Manufactured in the United States of America

CONTENTS

CONTENTS

SERIES FOREWORD

In response to high school and public library needs, Greenwood developed this distinguished series of full-length biographies specifically for student use. Prepared by field experts and professionals, these engaging biographies are tailored for high school students who need challenging yet accessible biographies. Ideal for secondary school assignments, the length, format and subject areas are designed to meet educators' requirements and students' interests.

Greenwood offers an extensive selection of biographies spanning all curriculum-related subject areas including social studies, the sciences, literature and the arts, history and politics, as well as popular culture, covering public figures and famous personalities from all time periods and backgrounds, both historic and contemporary, who have made an impact on American and/or world culture. Greenwood biographies were chosen based on comprehensive feedback from librarians and educators. Consideration was given to both curriculum relevance and inherent interest. The result is an intriguing mix of the well known and the unexpected, the saints and sinners from long-ago history and contemporary pop culture. Readers will find a wide array of subject choices from fascinating crime figures like Al Capone to inspiring pioneers like Margaret Mead, from the greatest minds of our time like Stephen Hawking to the most amazing success stories of our day like J.K. Rowling.

While the emphasis is on fact, not glorification, the books are meant to be fun to read. Each volume provides in-depth information about the subject's life from birth through childhood, the teen years, and adulthood. A thorough account relates family background and education, traces personal and professional influences, and explores struggles, accomplishments, and contributions. A timeline highlights the most significant life events against a historical perspective. Bibliographies supplement the reference value of each volume.

PREFACE

Christina Aguilera: A Biography provides current, honest, and interesting information about a hugely talented young woman who, through her tenacity and drive, carved out a career for herself in a world where the odds were stacked against her. The book is organized by the chronology of her life, starting in Chapter 1, "Beginnings," with the origins of her life, her parents—where they came from and how they met— her early life where she experienced the abuse of both herself and her mother, and how she turned that abuse into music. Chapter 2, "From Whence She Came," talks about her birthplace—Staten Island—and some of the unusual facts about that borough of New York. It also chronicles the world and national events of her early years, events that surely influenced her later views. Finally, it presents the history of music throughout the century and how it evolved into the music Aguilera eventually made. Chapter 3, "The Mouse That Roared," takes a close look at both the evolution of *The New Mickey Mouse Club* as well as Aguilera's days as a Mouseketeer. Chapter 4, "Becoming Good Christina," is about Aguilera's explosive breakthrough with her first album *Christina Aguilera* and the accompanying pain that went along with such instant success. Chapter 5, "Becoming Bad X-tina," talks

about the times surrounding her album *Stripped* and video "Dirrty."
Chapter 6, "Back to Basics," shows Aguilera's further evolution as she
modifies her wild style, meets her future husband, and launches yet
another success in her *Back to Basics* album. Chapter 7, "Finding True
Love," is a love story, sweet and simple. Chapter 8, "Motherhood,"
gives a very intimate view of Aguilera's new lifestyle and views after
the birth of her son, Max Liron. Finally, Chapter 9, "What's Ahead?"
presents a view of the very eclectic and busy life ahead as Aguilera begins a new phase of both her personal and professional lives.

In addition to a detailed chronicle and discussion of Aguilera's life
and career, the book also presents background material that augments
and provides perspective for a more in-depth understanding of Aguilera in a broader context of how her life and music have become a
product in a far greater scheme.

INTRODUCTION

Like the phases of the moon and the clouds that swirl by, Christina Aguilera has presented the world with a myriad of personas in the short span of her immensely successful career. First was the innocent child drowning the horrors of domestic abuse with a voice far beyond her tender years. Then there was the star of *The New Mickey Mouse Club*, wowing audiences with this very adult voice that could span four octaves and hit high E. This was followed by the lovely young woman with the wow-zow-powerful voice who was awarded a Grammy for Best New Artist in 2000. Next came the transformation to her sensuous, suggestive, and shocking self, first with the video "Lady Marmalade," followed by her vampy, seductive, and downright lascivious self in the album *Stripped*. Finally, her current image suggests a smoke-filled room ringing with sultry rhythm and blues, subtly sexy, a toned-down style motivated by her new life as wife and mother.

It is unquestionable that Christina's transformations have fascinated, shocked, delighted, and disgusted, but there is one thing no one can take away from her: her talent.

Standing about 20 rows back from the stage, Bob (a professional bodyguard) shakes his head. He's been working for Aguilera for just three months, after eight years with Madonna and six with Jennifer Lopez. "With those other girls, it was more about the show, the spectacle," Bob says. "But she"—he gestures up at Aguilera—"this one can sing."[1]

She's had her fights and she's had her detractors, but one thing everyone has to say about Christina Aguilera is indeed: "This one can sing."

Christina Maria Aguilera was born on December 18, 1980, in Staten Island, New York. She was the first child of Loraine Fidler Aguilera and Fausto Wagner Xavier Aguilera. Aguilera's early life was filled with world travels as her U.S. Army sergeant father's assignments required that the little family move from New York to Texas to New Jersey and then to Japan.

Aguilera's early childhood was bleakly colored with physical and emotional abuse, mostly directed at her mother, and this is where her passion for music emerged. Simply put, Aguilera took refuge in music. Not only did the sounds of her favorite album, *The Sound of Music*, drown out the yelling and crashing below, it served as the launching pad for a voice that has few equals.

Aguilera was an only child until her sister was born in 1986. It was a year after sister Rachel's birth before Aguilera's mother could no longer take the abuse. She then packed up her girls and fled to her mother's home in Rochester, Pennsylvania. It was during this time of newly found stability that Aguilera began to pester her mother to enter her in local talent contests, most of which she won. However, as a result of her success, or perhaps the attitude and confidence that went along with it, Aguilera began a long saga of being mocked and taunted by her classmates.

When she was nine, the producers of *The New Mickey Mouse Club* traveled the country auditioning to fill a precious few slots on the program. When they came to Pittsburgh, Aguilera was one of 400 children to try out. Against all odds, she made it into the top six but was subsequently rejected for being too young. Then at the age of 10 came the biggest contest of all when Aguilera was a contestant on *Star Search* singing Etta James's "A Sunday Kind of Love." However, this was also the first contest she lost. Not to be thwarted, she went on to compete in other contests earning such a reputation that when other contestants learned they'd be competing against her, they withdrew. She also appeared on hometown Pittsburgh radio programs and was repeatedly invited to all of Pittsburgh's major league team games to sing the National Anthem. It was at this time that she became known as "the little girl with the big voice."

Two years after Aguilera's audition for *The New Mickey Mouse Club*, her mother received a phone call from one of the producers who had kept her tapes from the previous audition to ask if Aguilera would be interested in trying out again. Of course the answer was yes, only this time Aguilera would have to audition against 15,000 children, nationwide. Aguilera made it into one of the just seven available slots. It was during this time that she met and worked with Britney Spears, with whom she would develop a love-hate relationship, and Justin Timberlake. Aguilera spent two years on the show until it shut down production in 1994.

In an attempt to jump-start her career since record deals were not as yet forthcoming, Aguilera traveled to Japan in 1997 where she recorded a duet and performed with Japanese pop star Keizo Nakanishi. After this she went on to Romania to represent the United States at the well-respected Golden Stag Festival.

Aguilera returned home and in early 1998, her life began happening. In January she recorded a series of demo discs, and in February she was sought after by the producers of Disney Studios to audition to sing the song "Reflection" from the movie *Mulan*. Aguilera got the deal and the next day she was in the studio. Just six months later, she signed a record deal with RCA Records and was soon into the recordings for her first album, *Christina Aguilera*, released in August 1999. Preceding the album by several weeks was the hit single "Genie in a Bottle," which catapulted to the top of the charts all over the world.

During 1999 she was courted everywhere and appeared on numerous television shows, specials, and even made a cameo appearance on the popular television show *90210*. Continuing on into 2000, the awards cascaded in with the pinnacle being her first Grammy Award, for Best New Artist. Aguilera was even named one of *Ladies' Home Journal's* women of the year.

After the release of *Christina Aguilera*, she began to explore her Latin roots, and so, in conjunction with well-respected Latin record producer Rudy Perez, she made the Spanish-language version of her first album, titled *Mi Reflejo*. Cashing in on the Latin pop craze, the album careened out the chute and debuted at number 27 in the United States. Soon after, she recorded the duet "Nobody Wants to Be Lonely" with fellow Latin performer, Ricky Martin. This single went on to be an international hit for which she won World's Best-Selling Female Latin Artist.

In 2001, Aguilera continued to rake in the awards, was coveted for the covers of numerous magazines, and began recording for her very controversial album *Stripped*. *Stripped* marked the emergence of her true self, Aguilera claimed. She had vehemently and publicly complained about the controlling natures of her management during her first album, and so she fired them and took on a new manager. She had felt controlled and manipulated into being a bubblegum princess by her previous management and was anxious to take control of her image and career.

Enter *Stripped*. The album itself, released in October 2002, was almost overshadowed by the controversial single "Dirrty" that thrilled, chilled, and/or disgusted fans throughout the world. The "Dirrty" video showed Aguilera in crotch-less chaps, dancing suggestively and flirting with male and female backup dancers alike.

After countless rumors over the years about her love life, in 2002 Aguilera began dating a young record producer from the Bronx named Jordan Bratman. Although they kept their courtship fairly discreet, the pair was married on November 19, 2005, under a setting sun in the hills of the Napa Valley.

Soon after their marriage, Aguilera was hard at work on her next album, *Back to Basics*. Released in August 2006, the double-disc album debuted at number one in the United States, United Kingdom, as well as 11 other countries.

Without a doubt, Aguilera's greatest accomplishment of all occurred on January 12, 2008, at 10:05 P.M.: the birth of her first child, son Max Liron Bratman, a name that means "our greatest song" in Latin and Hebrew. Since Bratman is Jewish, Aguilera agreed to celebrate all the Jewish holidays, which included Max's bris, a ceremony marking a baby boy's circumcision and naming.

Aguilera's values and lifestyle have drastically altered since mother-hood claimed her. She and Bratman bought a huge Hollywood home, complete with backyard recording studio so her morning and evening commutes have morphed into quick jaunts out the back door and back again, with several breaks during the day to play with her little Max. Her day-to-day routine has also changed. Formerly a night owl, prefer-ring to work well past the wee hours, she now insists on getting up with Max, which means a daily 6 A.M. wake-up call and bedtime at 12:30 A.M. Her desire to go out, party, and do anything without Max has dried up, at least for now. In fact, most paparazzi shots of Aguilera these days show her with Max safely and protectively ensconced in her arms.

Indeed, albeit with obviously new priorities, Aguilera has not aban-doned her work with a new album due out in 2010 as well as a movie, *Burlesque*, where she stars opposite Cher. There is also her charitable work with the World Hunger Relief Program and as spokesperson for a pro-voting campaign called Rock the Vote. Despite a daunting array of responsibilities, Aguilera has said she wants more children and that her family is her number one.

NOTE

1. "Christina Aguilera: Adult Swim," Blender.com, 2006, re-trieved December 14, 2009, from http://www.blender.com/guide/68 418/christina-aguilera-adult-swim.html.

TIMELINE: EVENTS IN THE LIFE OF CHRISTINA AGUILERA

December 18, 1980	Christina Maria Aguilera born in Staten Island University Hospital in Staten Island, New York, first child to Fausto Xavier Aguilera and Shelly Loraine Fidler Aguilera.
1982–1985	Her father is sergeant in the military; Christina's family is being moved around the world: Texas, Japan, and New Jersey.
1983–1985	Begins to take refuge in music to escape from family abuse; in particular, playing and singing to *The Sound of Music*.
June 6, 1986	Sister Rachel born.
1986	Shelly leaves Fausto and takes the girls to live with her mother in Rochester, Pennsylvania. Begins competing (and winning) in local talent shows where she incurs the jealousy of others in their small town.
1986–1993	Attends Rochester area elementary and middle schools.

1988   Competes in a talent contest singing Whitney
              Houston's "The Greatest Love of All" and her
              mother makes her shake the winner's hand
              when she loses.

March 15, 1990   Competes on *Star Search* singing "A Sunday
              Kind of Love" and loses.

1990   Sings same song on local radio program, *Wake
              Up with Larry Richert,* and people say she
              sounds 20.

1990–1993   Sings the "Star Spangled Banner" at Pittsburgh
              Steelers, Pittsburgh Pirates, and Pittsburgh
              Penguins games.

1992–1994   Joins *The New Mickey Mouse Club* and per-
              forms as a Mouseketeer along with Justin Tim-
              berlake and Britney Spears.

1993–1994   Attends North Allegheny High School in
              Wexford, Pennsylvania.

1997   Travels to Japan to record a duet with Keizo
              Nakanishi, one of Japan's most famous pop
              stars. Performs in Tokyo and travels to Ro-
              mania to represent the United States at the
              Golden Stag Festival, all to rave reviews.

January 1998 Begins recording demo discs and looking for
              record deals.

February 1998 Auditions to sing "Reflection" in the Disney
              animated film *Mulan*. Producers are looking
              for someone who could sing the high E above
              middle C. Wins the role and is in the studio a
              day later after making the deal.

June 1998   *Mulan* releases, also the single "Reflection,"
              which is nominated for a Golden Globe for
              Best Original Song in a Motion Picture. Ruth
              Inness hears Christina perform during a Disney
              practice and talks to Shelly about becoming
              Christina's manager. Christina is approached
              by Steve Kurtz to be her manager and signs a
              deal with Ron Fair of RCA for her first album.

August 1998	Recording on *Christina Aguilera* begins.
August 1999	"Genie in a Bottle" releases and hits No. 1 on the charts where it stays for five weeks.
	Travels with Lillith Fair.
August 24, 1999	*Christina Aguilera* releases and debuts at No. 1 on the Billboard chart.
September 1999	Makes cameo appearance on TV show *90210*.
October 1999	"Genie in a Bottle" releases in UK and immediately goes to top of charts.
November 1999	Performs on NBC-TV at Macy's Thanksgiving Day Parade.
December 1999	"What a Girl Wants" releases in United States and becomes first No. 1 single of 2000.
	Performs for President Clinton for Christmas, singing "The Christmas Song," as well as a duet with B. B. King; performance becomes a TV special called *Christmas in Washington*.
January 2000	Sings "I Turn to You" and "What a Girl Wants" at American Music Awards.
	Is chosen one of *Ladies' Home Journal*'s Women of the Year.
February 2000	Wins Grammy for Best New Artist.
April 2000	Appears on *Saturday Night Live* and episode wins an Emmy Award.
	Wins Best New Female Performer at Fifth Annual ALMA Awards.
May 2000	Wins awards for Favorite New Female Artist and Favorite Single ("Genie in a Bottle") at 2000 Blockbuster Awards.
	"Genie in a Bottle" is named International Hit of the Year at ASCAP Awards and also at Ivor Novello Awards.
June 2000	"Come on over Baby (All I Want Is You)" releases and reaches No. 1 on Billboard's Hot 100.
August 2000	Admits to being "in love" with Jorge Santos.

Records theme song for Coca-Cola ad campaign.

September 2000 Performs at MTV Awards where she is nominated for five awards: Best Female Video, Best Pop Video, Best New Artist, Viewer's Choice, and Best Choreography.

Mi Reflejo releases in United States and debuts at No. 27.

Performs at first annual Latin Grammys; is nominated for Best Female Pop Vocal Performance.

October 2000 *My Kind of Christmas* releases and debuts at No. 38 on the charts.

Fires manager Steve Kurtz for undue and inappropriate influence over her career.

Hires Irving Azoff as new manager.

December 2000 Stars in own TV special, *My Reflection*.

January 2001 *My Kind of Christmas* becomes certified Platinum.

Spring 2001 Demo disc, "Just Be Free," shows up in German record stores without contract or agreement.

March 2001 Records duet with Ricky Martin, "Nobody Wants to Be Lonely," that goes on to become international hit and for which she wins World's Best-Selling Female Latin Artist.

April 2001 Records remake version of "Lady Marmalade," from *Moulin Rouge* soundtrack, along with Pink, Mýa, and Lil' Kim; eventually becomes No. 1 on Billboard Hot 100.

July 2001 "Lady Marmalade" is nominated for seven MTV awards: Best Video, Best Dance Video, Best Pop Video, Best Video from a Film, Best Choreography in a Video, and Best Art Direction in a Video.

August 2001 Deal is made with Warlock Records to release album *Just Be Free* of her old demo tracks.

September 2001	"Lady Marmalade" wins Best Video of the Year and Best Video from a Film at the MTV Video Music Awards.
	Mi Reflejo achieves Gold, Platinum, and Triple Platinum status based on RIAA "Los Premios de Oro y Platino" guidelines.
October 26, 2001	Co-hosts 2001 Radio Music Awards with Ricky Martin.
November 2001	Wins Latin Grammy Award for Best Female Pop Vocal Album for *Mi Reflejo* and Record of the Year for "Pero Me Acuerdo De Ti."
December 2001	Wins Female Artist of the Year at Billboard Awards.
February 27, 2002	Christina, Lil' Kim, Mýa, and Pink win Grammy for Best Pop Collaboration with Vocals for "Lady Marmalade."
April 2002	Is nominated for five ALMA Awards.
	Appears on the cover of *Allure* magazine.
August 2002	Shooting for "Dirrty" video begins and the single "Dirrty" releases.
October 22, 2002	*Stripped* releases, selling 330,000 in first week.
Late 2002	Begins dating Jordan Bratman.
June 2003	Joins Justin Timberlake on what becomes *Justified and Stripped* tour.
August 2003	Famous kiss among Madonna, Britney Spears, and Christina occurs at inaugural MTV Video Music Award ceremony.
2004	Is featured on billboards for "Only You Can Make a Difference" to increase voter registration for November presidential elections.
January 2004	*Zoo* magazine reports that Christina might be bisexual.
Summer 2004	Her own tour is scrapped because of injuries to vocal chords.
February 2005	Announces engagement to Jordan Bratman.
August 2005	Album *Possibilities* releases, in which Christina collaborates with Herbie Hancock for

	recording "A Song for You." Song goes on to be nominated for Grammy for Best Pop Collaboration with Vocals.
November 19, 2005	Marries Jordan Bratman.
March 2006	Signs contract with Orange, European cell phone company, to represent the company.
May 2006	Poses nude for GQ magazine.
August 15, 2006	Double-CD album *Back to Basics* releases and debuts at No. 1 in the United States, UK, and 11 other countries.
Late 2006	Begins *Back to Basics* European tour.
2007	Fragrance "Christina Aguilera" is introduced in Europe.
September 9, 2007	Attends party where Paris Hilton publicly congratulates, and thus reveals, Christina's pregnancy.
September 16, 2007	Performs with Tony Bennett at 59th Emmy Awards Ceremony.
Late 2007	Becomes spokesperson for Rock the Vote, young people's awareness program for 2008 elections.
January 12, 2008, at 10:05 P.M.	Gives birth to first child, son Max Liron Bratman.
January 2008	Sells Max's baby pictures to *People* magazine for $1,500,000.
Mid-2008	Makes public service announcements for Rock the Vote. Is involved with Macy's 150th anniversary program. Next fragrance "Inspire" releases in United States.
November 11, 2008	Special album sold only through Target releases, *Keeps Gettin' Better: A Decade of Hits*.
July 15, 2009	Is named global spokesperson for Yum! Brands World Hunger Relief program.

August 7, 2009	Launches her own radio station on *iheartradio* network.
Late 2009	Third fragrance "Christina Aguilera by Night" releases.
June 2010	Fourth album *Bionic* releases.
November 2010	Expected release of first acting/movie role: *Burlesque*.

Chapter 1

BEGINNINGS

December 18, 1980, was a typically cold winter's day in Staten Island, New York. Despite the cold, the winds were light and the skies clear[1] as the first piercing cries of a newborn baby girl named Christina Maria Aguilera echoed through the maternity wards of Staten Island University Hospital.[2] Surely everyone thought this was just another crying baby, albeit with a cry louder than some, but little did they know *this* cry was the foreshadowing of the stunning voice that would one day follow and literally captivate the world.

Aguilera was the first child of Shelly Loraine Fidler, who was 20 when Aguilera was born, and Fausto Wagner Xavier Aguilera, 12 years older than Fidler. Aguilera's mother was born in the United States on March 23, 1960, to Delcie Fidler who came to the United States directly from Ireland. Fidler spoke Spanish fluently due to her education in the language during college, and thus, she worked as a translator. Besides her fluency and work in Spanish, Fidler was a musician in her own right and perhaps this was where Aguilera's musical spark turned wildfire originated. Fidler was a talented violinist and piano player who had her own moments of fame. In a move where history would one day repeat itself, Fidler's mother encouraged her young daughter to showcase her talents and travel the world.[3] And so, due to this encouragement, at age 16 Fidler traveled throughout Europe, playing with the Youth Symphony Orchestra. The line of strong Fidler women began with Delcie Fidler, whose husband died when her daughter was just 12. And so she carried on, raising her children and running a household—alone. This strength was passed onto Aguilera's mother who, after escaping the brutality of her husband, became a single mother to two young girls. In fact, during Aguilera's Mouseketeer days, she was voted the No. 2 best showbiz mom by *In Touch* magazine, falling just behind Justin Timberlake's mom, Lynn Harless.[4]

Aguilera's father was born in Guayaquil, Ecuador, came to the United States, and subsequently served as a sergeant in the U.S. Army. Accounts differ about the place of Shelly and Fausto's meeting, but what is confirmed is that two people, one by the name of Shelly Aguilera, and the other, Fausto Aguilera, both attended Brigham Young University in 1979.[5] It is also documented that the two were married at the LDS (Latter Day Saints) Chapel in Washington, D.C.[6] The Church of the Latter Day Saints has been a factor in Ecuadoran religious life since 1965, with a mission established in Guayaquil in 1966. It is possible that Aguilera brought his religion with him to the United States and was responsible for converting Fidler from Catholicism.

Further investigation by Pete Thunell, editor of BYU News Net (Brigham Young University), yielded some evidence that Aguilera was exposed to, if not practiced, the Mormon faith. He discovered that both a "Fausto Aguilera" and a "Shelly Aguilera" attended Brigham Young University in 1979. Following this discovery was yet another involving Aguilera's alleged home teacher, named Tom Duty, who evidently taught her when she was nine years old and living in Pennsylvania. However, Duty also conjectured that Aguilera probably would not remember either him or the church.[7]

Other accounts have Aguilera's parents meeting in Newfoundland while her father was stationed at Harmon Air Force Base in Stephensville. However, there is no account that Fidler was there during that time. Since Aguilera was born in 1980, it is plausible that her parents met earlier while they were allegedly in Newfoundland and then traveled to Utah where they both attended college. What is known is that Fidler was always profoundly intrigued with the Latino culture and studied the Spanish language and culture in preparation to become a translator. Wherever they met, it is likely that Aguilera's father's Latin heritage attracted his soon-to-be young bride and that even though raised Catholic, she followed him to the Church of the Latter Day Saints' Brigham Young University. Following their time at Brigham Young University, Fausto Aguilera's military career took the couple to Staten Island, during which time Christina was born. Soon after her birth, his career took the family around the world on a number of army assignments, including to Texas, Florida, Japan, and New Jersey.[8]

Although these were Aguilera's early years, surely there were some indelible effects on her psyche as a developing child. The term "Army brat" is deserving in the effects it has on children, not the least of which is a missing sense of place as families are hurtled from place to place with as little as a few scant months in some assignments.[9] Also intrinsic to army life, especially when families were housed on the base, was the well-known rigid, authoritarian, and highly disciplined lifestyle. On the positive side were adaption skills that came from the instability of such a lifestyle: "There are worse things than being unable to explain yourself or having a rambling childhood. You adapt. You learn."[10] There is no question but that this lifestyle affected Aguilera profoundly, both in her rejection of rigidity as well as her highly honed adaptation skills, which would serve her well as she encountered the many rocks that littered her future path.

THE UGLY STUFF

Long before Aguilera began her trek to stardom, the little Aguilera family embarked on a twisting and painful downhill slide filled with ugliness and abuse. The journey on this road to verbal and physical abuse was horrible for young Aguilera, who sometimes intervened in futile efforts to save her mother from her father's terrible rages. However, to cope she was more likely to run to her room where she'd play *The Sound of Music* and sing as loud as she could along with her heroine, Julie Andrews, to drown out the sounds of the violence below.

Although it was the catalyst for the start of her musical career, the abuse clearly left deep scars. Aguilera has openly admitted that her strong drive and passion is a product of her youth and the abuse that defined it with music giving Aguilera her only tranquil escape:

> My earliest memories are definitely of singing "Sound of Music." When I discovered Julie Andrews and "The Sound of Music," I immediately fell in love. I had the soundtrack on a little tape. I'd put it in my boombox in my room, and I would just, like, close my door and open my window and just sing out. I don't know. It was such a release for me, growing up, for any bad energy or anything that was going on, tension or pain that I was going through. Singing was a way of releasing that. It made me really happy. I would just sing that all over the place.[11]

What caused the strife and turmoil between Aguilera's parents? Perhaps it was the mixture of her father's hot Latin blood with her mother's comparatively cool Anglican blood that triggered the rages, although Fidler was also rumored to have had a temper of her own. Or maybe it was their age difference. Or perhaps it was the constant moving. More likely a combination of these and other factors made the lives of the Aguileras increasingly turbulent during Christina Aguilera's first five years. But whatever it was, the damage was done and Aguilera today admits to never feeling safe while growing up. "Growing up I did not feel safe. Feeling powerless is the worst feeling in the world."[12]

The military life is also a hotbed for family abuse, probably because of its rigidity and authoritarianism. Anything, including the behavior of normal spouses and children, could be catalysts for violence of either or both a physical and sexual nature. A study of Navy families found that between 29 and 52 percent of children were victimized by abuse in their families.[13] Then there is also the question of alcohol abuse. For 20 years, officials in all branches of the military have struggled to lower the alarmingly high rate—21 percent—of heavy drinking admitted to by enlisted men and women. Surely the rate is even higher and therefore a significant issue.[14] Could Aguilera's father have been a notch in the belt of this statistic?

Aguilera remained an only child until 1986 when her sister Rachel was born. Although the familial abuse continued after the baby's birth, Aguilera's mother tried desperately to keep the family together until she could take it no more. In a 2009 documentary on *E!*, Aguilera and her mother Fidler talked extensively about the past and Aguilera's childhood. One incident in particular stood out for both mother and daughter, and that was when Aguilera was four, she disturbed her father from a nap. He got up, flew into a rage, and attacked her. Fidler discovered Aguilera covered in blood, and scooped up her daughter and asked what happened. Fidler reported that Aguilera mumbled, "Daddy wanted to take a nap and I made too much noise."[15] It was then that Fidler knew she'd hit the end of the road with her husband.

As quickly as she could, Fidler amassed the money necessary to pack herself and her girls together and drive to her mother's house in Rochester, Pennsylvania, a small town north of Pittsburgh. Delcie Fidler indeed provided a safe haven for her daughter and granddaughters for several years.

When all was said and done, Aguilera's father denied his alleged cruelty and abuse but did admit that he and Fidler were fiery during their marriage.

> My relationship with her [Aguilera's] mother was tense and I wasn't perfect. But I love Christina and her sister.
>
> I never abused them in any way and they know that. Shelly and I disagreed on a lot of things and we both had hot tempers.
>
> I'm sorry to have ever raised a hand to my wife, but it was never brutal like Ike and Tina Turner. Still, even though it's been exaggerated, I respect Shelly and Christina's right to remember things differently.[16]

Despite its horrors, Aguilera said, "You can either repeat the cycle or react against it, as I have done."[17] And react against it she has indeed done, going back to the age of three when Fidler tells of people stopping in shock at the singing voice coming from her little girl. Fidler said: "I could basically tell from a very young age that this was sort of out of my hands. It was out of my hands. It was literally something that she seemed like she was born to do."[18] And so, even though separated from her father and the screaming arguments that ravaged her early life, Aguilera continued her singing and love of music.

CHILD PRODIGY

Soon after Fidler and her girls moved to Rochester, the young Aguilera's grandmother began to notice her granddaughter's amazing voice. Fidler, still consumed with the emotional and financial aspects of the breakup of her marriage, had not tuned in to her daughter's talent, at least not to its full and robust extent. With her mother's encouragement, as well as young Aguilera's urging, it became clear to Fidler that it was contest time. Starting at age six, Aguilera begged her mother to enter her in local talent contests, and she also participated in school contests. Always the winner and confident in her abilities, there was, however, a price to pay for this fledgling success and that was the taunting and mocking by her classmates. In fact, this was a price she would pay right up into adulthood. Yet Aguilera, ever stalwart, marched forth, undeterred from her goal to one day become a famous singer. Clearly her tremendous focus later in life comes from these early years where she exhibited strength of character unusual for a child. As well, her profound confidence must also have emerged from standing true to her passions and eschewing the taunts of her classmates.

In one contest, eight-year-old wunderkind Aguilera sang Whitney Houston's "Greatest Love of All" and competed against a 12-year-old young fellow who sang Eddie Holman's "Hey There Lonely Girl." His performance was indeed memorable, and he won the competition. She said: "I was a good sport about it. My Mom made me go out and shake his hand and tell him I was happy he won. Tears were running down my face. Awful."[19]

While her classmates continued taunting her, Aguilera continued galloping down the path of her exploding career. At age 10 (1990), she became a contestant on the program *Star Search*, singing Etta James's "A Sunday Kind of Love," marking her first national television appearance. *Star Search* was also the launching pad of fellow cohorts in crime and entertainment, Britney Spears who wowed the audience at age 10 (1991) and Justin Timberlake (also 1991). For Aguilera, it was 8 going on 18 with her sexy, sultry moves already captivating audiences while her multioctave voice stunned them into silent disbelief. Did she win? No. Was she thwarted? Perhaps disappointed, but thwarted, absolutely not. Never thwarted.

After her loss on *Star Search*, Aguilera applied to become a contestant on a local Pittsburgh talent show called *Jude Pohl's Talent Showcase*, and, of course, she was accepted right away. This time she won the competition. Said Jude Pohl, theatrical producer for the Pittsburgh show:

> It wasn't that she had a big voice . . . She had an adult voice. We could have had her compete in the adult female vocalist contest if she'd been behind a curtain.[20]

Her talent then began to precede her and the 11-year-old prodigy went on to compete in other contests and it became well known that if Aguilera was a contestant, other entrants withdrew. The word continued to spread and also at 11, she was invited to perform at a Pittsburgh area charity event. The audience was so amazed at the little girl/big voice combination that she received invitations to sing the national anthem at Pittsburgh professional sports events, including the Steelers, Penguins, and Pirates games. In this capacity, she was the youngest person to ever perform at a national sports event, and she went on to sing at these events for several years. Aguilera was also a well-known voice on local radio programs, and she indeed became known as "the little girl with the big voice."

TAUNTS FROM KIDS

Still, back on the home front, the taunting and jeering from Aguilera's classmates, born from their jealousy of Aguilera's talent and self-assurance, which the other children most likely interpreted as snobbery or conceit, continued. In fact, it escalated to the point where her mother's tires were slashed and another child attempted to assault Aguilera during gym class.[21]

So it became time to move . . . again. Because of the daunting violence and Aguilera's increasing fame, Fidler was discrete about the move. She took her girls and moved to Wexford, Pennsylvania, another suburb of Pittsburgh, where at age 11 Aguilera entered the sixth grade at Marshall Middle School.

HOMETOWN, USA

Was there also something about the place where Aguilera spent most of her childhood that gave fodder to her brilliant singing career? Who knows, but what is known is that Wexford is an interesting little town located near Pittsburgh that was once ranked number 28 on the CNN-Money.com list of Best Places. The ranking criteria were for cities with populations higher than 14,000 and with above-average income, steady population growth, and significant appreciation in real estate. In other words, places that demonstrated economic growth and upward mobility.[22] Still, the town has many upper-middle-class residents. Route 19 is the main thoroughfare and it hosts a bevy of corporate chains and car dealerships. Social life in the town revolved around school activities. In fact, Aguilera's high school, North Allegheny Senior High School, otherwise known as NASH, is recognized to be one of the best schools in the state. In addition to educationally based social life, residents also engage one another in the many coffee shops and restaurants that are dotted throughout the town. It is clearly a typical, upscale American suburb. But, in considering the demographics of the town, it is clear that Aguilera's family was not in the upper-middle-class league and one cannot help but wonder if this was a factor in her problems with classmates growing up.

She never became popular, even in her new schools, and she would later explain that the other children simply could not understand her tremendous focus and drive for her singing. However, on the other hand, was the trouble with her peers the start of a trend that would follow her into adulthood? In other words, what was her part, if any, in the never-ending issues she had with peers?

At last, after Aguilera's first year of high school and after years of dealing with the taunts and petty jealousies of her high school classmates, Fidler decided to pull Aguilera from public school and began to home school her. This gave Aguilera more time and flexibility to nurture her career, and when she wasn't studying, she worked on her first album, *Christina Aguilera*. Despite her absence from high school, in the spring of 1999, Aguilera attended the senior ball at her former high school, North Allegheny High School. Originally not intending to go, she showed up with a date on each arm. But as usual, the girls all ignored her while the boys flocked like bees to a flower.

"My peers couldn't relate to the things I was doing outside school, and that was always going to create resentment and anxiety," Aguilera said.[23]

That was until she burst forth into a new world as a Mouseketeer where she was surrounded by like-minded young people.

"For the first time I was with kids who were as passionate about the same things as me," she said.[24]

A GROWING FAMILY

After several years of single parenthood, Shelly Aguilera met and married a wonderful man and a paramedic, Jim Kearns. However, during their courtship, and in the early years of their marriage, Aguilera was distrustful and somewhat resentful of her stepfather. But after several years she came to trust and even love this man whom she would thank as her father when she received her first Grammy Award.

The Kearns were married on May 12, 1991, and suddenly Aguilera had two additional siblings, a stepsister named Stephanie, age five, and a stepbrother named Casey, age seven. Five years after their marriage, the Kearns also had a child of their own, Michael. In the meantime, Aguilera and Rachel remained close, albeit with Rachel remaining most gracefully in the background as her sister's career soared. As the years went on, Aguilera would take comfort in playing "Super Mario Brothers" together and generally having fun just "hanging out."[25]

Given the simple facts, one cannot help but wonder about Aguilera's emotional response to suddenly being faced with an exploding family. First, she had been an only child for the first six years of her life, so just the birth of her sister must have dealt a shock of having to suddenly share her mother's time and affection. Then came the ready-made family with two additional siblings and a stepfather, a man now intrinsic in her life after her previous experience with men had been so traumatic. In addition, her mother fully took on the role of mother to her stepchildren, undoubtedly diluting her focus on Aguilera even more. Where did this leave Aguilera? Most likely she directed more energy into her career and perhaps began a healthy process of becoming more independent and self-reliant while still knowing familial support was there if she needed it.

NOTES

1. Pier Dominguez, *Christina Aguilera: A Star Is Made* (Phoenix: Colossus Books, 2003), http://www.almanac.com/weatherhistory/oneday.php?number=744976&wban=99999&day=18&month=12&year=1980&searchtype=.

2. Dr. Thomas Mateo, "Women of Staten Island," *Staten Island Historian*, 2008, retrieved October 8, 2009 from http://www.statenisland historian.com/Women_of_Staten_Island.html.

3. Dominguez, *Christina Aguilera*, p. 2.

4. "Christina Aguilera," Imdb.com, retrieved July 6, 2010, from http://www.imdb.com/name/nm0004694/bio.

5. Pete Thunell, "Here's the Skinny on LDS Celebrity Urban Legends," Universe.byu.edu, retrieved July 6, 2010, from http://newsnet.byu.edu/story.cfm/12627.

6. "Christina Aguilera," Imdb.com.

7. Thunell, "Here's the Skinny on LDS Celebrity Urban Legends."

8. Dominguez, *Christina Aguilera*, 2.

9. Michael Hall, "Army Brat," *Texas Monthly*, December 2005.

10. Ibid., 28th paragraph retrieved December 3, 2009, from http://www.texasmonthly.com/2005-12-01/feature2-1.php.

11. Ed Masley, "Blessed by a 'Genie,'" *Pittsburgh Post-Gazette*, August 13, 1999, retrieved March 3, 2010, from http://www.postgazette.com/magazine/19990813christina1.asp.

12. Moira Holden, "Aguilera Talks about Dad's 'Abuse,'" UKfamily.co.uk, retrieved September 24, 2009, from http://ukfamily.co.uk/life style/news/2009-9/general/Christina-aguilera-dad-abuse.html.

13. Doug Brunk, "Children in Navy Families Report Child Abuse in Study," *Family Practice News*, June 15, 2001, 32.

14. Staff Sgt. Kathleen T. Rhem, USA, American Forces Press Service, "Alcohol Abuse Costs DoD Dearly," About.com: US Military, June 6, 2000, retrieved March 19, 2010, from http://usmilitary.about.com/library/milinfo/milarticles/blalcohol.htm.

15. Holden, "Aguilera Talks about Dad's 'Abuse.'"

16. Ibid.

17. Adrian Thrills, "Britney? I Wish Her All the Best . . . Honest!," *Daily Mail* (London), November 7, 2008.

18. Masley, "Blessed by a 'Genie.'"

19. Anthony Bozza, "The Christina Aguilera Story (so far)," *Rolling Stone*, October 28, 1999.

20. Masley, "Blessed by a 'Genie,'" para 51.

21. "Christina Aguilera," Celebspin.com, retrieved July 6, 2010, from http://www.celebspin.com/2006/07/Christina-aguilera/.

22. Wexford, PA, CNNMoney.com, retrieved July 6, 2010, from http://money.cnn.com/magazines/moneymag/bplive/2005/snapshots/36839.html.

23. Thrills, "Britney?"

24. Ibid.

25. "Family," retrieved February 24, 2010, from http://www.xtina-web.com/family.php.

Chapter 2

FROM WHENCE SHE CAME

STATEN ISLAND LEGACIES

Aguilera was preceded by a long line of strong, powerful, and talented women who either were born or had their base in Staten Island. Renowned folk singer Joan Baez was born there in 1941. Gloria Cordes-Elliot, the real-life inspiration for the movie A League of Their Own and winning pitcher in women's All-Star Baseball from 1950–1954, was also born in Staten Island. Another Staten Islander and sports star, Jen Derevjanik, went on to play in the Women's National Basketball League and helped her team, Phoenix Mercury, go on to victory. On the artistic side, there was Ann Duquesnay, who won a Tony Award for her role in the Broadway production of Bring in 'Da Noise, Bring in 'Da Funk, as well as actor Jennifer Esposito whose notable role was in the television show Spin City. Another show business Staten Island native is Alyssa Milano, who besides her well-known role in Who's the Boss, opposite Tony Danza, also had the title role in a touring company of the Broadway show Annie. Although there were others, the last to mention is the famous Jenny Lind, the blonde butterfly brought from Sweden to the United States and hired by P. T. Barnum in 1850 on a two-year contract[1] and who ended up settling in Staten Island. Also in the entertainment realm, the following movies were all filmed in Staten Island: *The Godfather* (1972), *Scent of a Woman* (1992), and *Descent* (2007).

Of New York City's five boroughs, Staten Island remains the smallest in population with approximately 487,000 inhabitants and a total land mass of 102.5 square miles. In contrast, when Aguilera was born, the population was 352,000. It is also by far the most typically suburban of the New York City boroughs. It boasts a beach boardwalk: the F.D.R. Boardwalk, which at two and a half miles long, is the fourth-longest boardwalk in the world. The breakdown of the current population is Italian: 34 percent, Irish: 14 percent, African American: 10 percent, Puerto Rican: 6 percent, German: 6 percent, Polish: 4 percent, Russian: 3 percent, and all others: 23 percent.[2]

The first note of civilization in Staten Island occurred in 1524 when Giovanni da Verrazano arrived, dropping anchor off shore for a very short period of time. The 1800s was a colorful time for the island. First, and also a recent discovery, was a housing community called Sandy Ground inhabited by a group of free blacks who settled on the island before the Civil War. A mostly black-attended church currently sits in the middle of a mostly white area of 150-year-old Sandy Ground homes.[3] Also in the 1800s, the New York City area in general underwent the influx of huge numbers of immigrants and Staten Island was the location of quarantine housing. Stupidly, the nursing staff for the facility had no restrictions on their comings and goings, thus acting as veritable Petri dishes of germs and infection. The people of Staten Island complained and complained, but nothing was done about it, at least not by local authorities. Finally, the people took matters into their own hands and they burned down the germ-ridden facility in 1858.[4]

Despite the island's interesting past and rather pleasant quality of life, due to Fausto Aguilera's military career, the family moved from Staten Island shortly after Aguilera's birth and so she probably does not remember much, if anything, about it.

THE WORLD AT HER FINGERTIPS

Aguilera's early years were accompanied by significant changes in the nation's culture. Status was the watchword as the country segued into the "Me, Me, Me!" Generation. The parade of the rich and famous was heralded by Donald Trump, the renowned real estate mogul, Leona Helmsley of the hotel fame, and Ivan Boesky, master of buyouts, mergers, and hostile takeovers. Following their lead, people clamored for credit cards and debt was incurred like candy. It was all about style, labels, designer clothes, and big shiny cars. Only beneath the style, labels, designer clothes, and big cars was the naked truth that the perceived wealth was simply a house of cards.[5]

Jimmy Carter was president for one year before Ronald Reagan, who was president from 1981–1989. The rabid shopping frenzy of the decade poised Reagan to necessarily deal with double-digit inflation as well as rising unemployment, which led to a recession early in his presidency. Also during his tenure, he embarked upon the journey that would precipitate the end of the cold war that had plagued the nation and terrified its citizens for many years. As well, this was also the time that the Berlin Wall finally cracked, forever changing the world because of the collapse of communism. The Sunbelt was in its sunny glory during the decade as people relocated from the north in droves for the promise of employment and better weather. It was also a time during which the United States had its 200th birthday celebration, which sent its citizens into a frenzy of celebratory pride in their country. Unfortunately, the explosion of the space shuttle *Challenger* (1986), and with it the death of teacher Christa McAuliffe, also marked this decade and served as a grim wake-up call to man's potential fallibility in space.[6]

Despite its failure in space, technology nevertheless exploded during these years: main frames in climate-controlled rooms morphed into desktops that resided in family rooms. AIDS was at its terrifying peak while scientists scrambled to find a cure. The Super Mario Brothers' familiar tag-melody echoed throughout homes across the country, and women began making inroads with Sandra Day O'Connor as the first woman on the Supreme Court and Geraldine Ferraro as the first woman candidate for U.S. president. Thus Aguilera would enter into a world where women had gone before and begun to chip away at a male-dominated and chauvinistic culture.

This was also the decade of fast food: its exponential growth accompanied the beginning of the soccer-mom era where kids flocked to team sports and their mothers went crazy trying to keep track of games, scores, and last and often least—homework. Sweetarts, Nerds, Skittles, and bubble gum kept kids quiet and happily chewing as the traditional dinner hour dwindled to fast-food-on-the-run fare. In fact, fast food was to become Aguilera's food of choice.

Fashion grew funky with women's hair boasting blonde galore, crimping, feathering, and lots of glitter. For the men it was the Mohawk, the long and layered look, and the long-haired ponytail. Makeup for women was heavy, with tons of mascara, a preponderance of blue eye shadow, and light pink lips. Men sported a punk look with piercings on their face and Ray-Ban sunglasses even in the dark. For women, the miniskirt was back, along with cropped tops, big belts, and long T-shirts. Men donned Ocean Pacific T-shirts, lots of chains on leather, and rolled sleeves. Jeans were tight on both men and women, while women wore legwarmers, exercise outfits, and spandex. Corduroy, parachute, and leather pants were hot for the men. Accessories were abundant on women with hoop earrings, slouchy socks, and rubber bracelets the standouts. For men it was Croc Dundee hats and high-top sneaks. Branding was big and you were only cool if clothes came from Ocean Pacific, Liz Claiborne, Banana Republic, and the Gap for women; Jordache, Guess, and Izod for the guys. Finally, the decade was chock full of trends including boom boxes (Aguilera was later to record her mega-successful demo tapes on a boom box), skateboarding, break dancing, Cabbage Patch dolls, and video arcades. In other words, for young people, it was a decade full of fun, funky, and frivolity in fashion, style, and trends.[7]

As for the decade's numbers, 70 percent of Americans owned a home in 1987 and the average price of a home in 1985 was $84,300. Renters paid an average of $400 per month. The workers of the decade were mostly white collar, 55 percent working at jobs including managerial, professional, sales, or technical. This was the era in which large companies nurtured large and lifelong workforces. In 1986, General Motors employed 811,000, Sears Roebuck & Company was next with 409,000. IBM employed 405,000, Ford Motor Company, 369,000, and last, AT&T with 337,000. The average family income in 1987 was $30,853 and families making $86,000 were in the top 5 percent income bracket. Also in 1987, 30 percent of the cars in America were imports, and the average price of a car was $12,585. Most popular were Ford Escort, Ford

Taurus, and Honda Accord. Love was in the air in the 1980s as well, though this was well before the days of online dating. The most common meeting vehicles were through friends or social gatherings. Single parenthood was the norm in some segments of society with 42 percent of white children and 86 percent of black children living with just one parent. Abuse in families was still a major factor, but there was also a decline in violent abuse due to tougher penalties for those convicted. Children of the 1980s were sadly underfit and only 2 percent of them passed the 1984 Presidential Physical Fitness test. Television consumed an enormous amount of people's leisure time with 82 percent of adults watching television every day. Likewise, seven hours was the average amount of time most homes had the television on daily. Plays were attended by 67 percent Americans once each year, while concerts were attended by 60 percent.

The 1980s was the decade when many very serious issues found themselves in the homes of the average American, instead of irrelevant stories in the morning newspaper. No matter what the party or religious affiliation, most agreed that sex education should be taught in the public schools. The reason for this generalized agreement was, it was hoped, to lower the predominance of unwanted teen pregnancies. Smoking was on the wane, falling to 30 percent after a 1950s maximum of 45 percent. The National Rifle Association was in a position of power with the support of President Reagan behind it, and in general, it was a decade where the balance of power was tipped toward conservatism. But on the other hand, the American people wanted more control over guns, a figure of 60 percent in a 1986 survey. The media, specifically movies and magazines that were on the sexually explicit side, were seen to be the scourge of society causing a breakdown of public morality. A whopping 67 percent of those surveyed were in favor of limiting such material.[8]

In music, the changes in this decade were staggering. The most notable developments were the introduction of MTV and the compact disc. MTV became known as "illustrated radio."[9] It was also the last decade of the megahit single where songs were much bigger hits than they are today. Why? The sale of singles started their downward slide because the potential of the Internet for music was already on the horizon.[10] In addition, the range of music genres expanded greatly to include heavy metal, new wave, rap, techno pop, alternative rock, and a changed country sound.[11] Of course, the list of hits is long with some of the more notables including "Magic," by Olivia Newton John, "Rock with You," by Michael Jackson, "Working My Way Back to You—Forgive Me Girl," The Spinners, "Please Don't Go," K. C. & and The Sunshine Band, "Sailing," by Christopher Cross, and "Passion," by Rod Stewart.

FROM LINDY HOP TO HOT POP

Did the world at the time instill into Aguilera a passion so clearly focused at the tender age of three? And how aware and affected was she by the dramatic events of the decade? Ironically her experience with music parallels the history of pop, a history that is as eclectic and interesting as she is. But first, a definition of terms: is pop music short for popular music? No. As defined by the *New Grove Dictionary of Music and Musicians*,[12] popular music is music produced since the Industrial Revolution that is written to appeal to the urban middle class. The scope of popular music is quite broad and ranges from the music accompanying old silent movies to the heavy metal sounds of Led Zeppelin and Van Halen.

Pop, on the other hand, is music for the masses, produced to be available and appeal to all as opposed to just the urban middle class. Taking it to its roots, working in what was dubbed as the Golden Era, artists of the 1930s and 1940s, such as Irving Berlin and George Gershwin, were indeed the pop music writers of their time. Why? Berlin hoped that his music would reach everyone, and Gershwin was committed to writing music that would be available to and delight the masses. He even went so far as to call *Porgy and Bess* a folk opera instead of an opera for just this reason.[13]

A characteristic of this early pop is that most of it was written by songwriters for performers, often for those who performed in musical comedy stage productions, as opposed to today's pop, which is both written and performed by the singers themselves. For example, some of the famous songwriters of the time wrote their best-known works specifically for Fred Astaire who sang them perfectly. These writers included Irving Berlin, Jerome Kern, Dorothy Fields, and the Gershwins,[14] and they knew exactly how to write to make both their music, and Fred's performances, sound magnificent!

The music of the Golden Age was fun, sing- and dance-able, light, and appealing to most audiences. These were tunes that listeners didn't think much about, other than to whistle happy tunes under their breath while strolling down the street. The music made people feel good. It wasn't deep and not particularly meaningful.

The inception of modern pop actually evolved from 1950s rock and roll, most notably, the music of generational icon Elvis Presley. Presley's music served as the bridge between the Golden Age and current forms of pop because it was still written by separate songwriters specifically to be performed by him. On the other hand, this form of pop became known as rock and roll, which was another building block in the further evolution of music. The next step was an untainted form of pop, which emerged in the 1960s, thanks to the likes of Bob Dylan, John Lennon, and Paul McCartney.

> This situation changed as a revolution occurred in popular music. Within a few years in the middle of the decade, popular songwriting was transformed from an experimental to a conceptual art. This changed not only the locus of the creation of popular songs, as professional songwriters were replaced by singer-songwriters but also the form and substance of popular music. Today, more than four decades later, the conceptual approach to popular songwriting remains dominant.[15]

The new pop had a form of its own, which was generally a series of different verses punctuated by a single chorus. The songs were typically three to six minutes long and exhibited a combination of disco, rhythm and blues, hip-hop, country, and rock. In addition, this new form of pop segued from performers who were fine craftsmen in performing other people's works to artists who created and performed their own musical works. These emerging singer-songwriters created pieces that were introspective and self-absorbed, claiming that they wrote their music without care to what the general populace thought. As Dylan said: "I don't care what people say."[16] With much of it dark, this music of the masses was very different from the light and airy music of the Golden Age.

HOW DID AGUILERA FIT IN?

Enter the era of eclectic music. The 1980s ushered in the phenomenon of MTV, the CD, and a new form of movement called break dancing, a form introduced and perhaps perfected by Michael Jackson. During this time there were many forms of music in both the United States and the world, including pop, rock, country, and in the late 1980s—rap joined the lineup.

MTV, or music TV, gave singers, songwriters, and musicians an incredible new platform to combine the visual with sound for an effect that wowed audiences and catapulted performers into instant stardom. It was a phenomenon that had no equal up to that time. Owned by Viacom, it was, and still is, the primary music television channel in the world.[17]

Many were one-hit wonders who quickly sank into oblivion, but others rose to the top where they still remain. In this latter category are Madonna, Michael Jackson, until his death, and Phil Collins. At the same time, a harder core rock evolved with the likes of Van Halen and Aerosmith. The musical pool into which Aguilera would dive was formidable, but the opportunities for exposure were seemingly made for her form of art, and artist is what she certainly became.

This was the then morphing stage onto which Aguilera would later dominate, especially when she broke free of restraint in management and took control of her own art and image. Shadowing her musical forbearers, Aguilera, with her music exhibiting notes of rhythm and blues, hip-hop, pop, and more, followed the likes of Dylan with his music, which was an interesting mix of folk, blues, country, rhythm and blues, gospel, and rock and roll.

Consider writer David Galenson's statement:

a classic example of a conceptual innovation made by young, inexperienced artists who are concerned with creating new art forms and have little regard for, or knowledge of, traditional rules and constraints: their inexperience can effectively limit them

from conventions that constrain more experienced or more respectful artists.[18]

Does this refer to Aguilera? It surely could, but it was in fact written
about the Beatles and their classic hit, "Strawberry Fields," and is a
commentary on the bravery evident in the unconventional approaches
to the music of the time, bravery that would certainly characterize
Aguilera as her art matured.

LATIN POP

It's important to discuss Latin pop because of both Aguilera's ethnic-
ity and her foray into the genre. The origin of the genre comes from
two factions. First is simply regular pop music sung in a romance language, mainly Spanish and Portuguese. The second is not pure pop,
instead mixing more traditional Latin forms, such as salsa, tango, fla-
menco, reggae, and more. Ritchie Valens is noted to be the Latin pop
voice heard around the world with his hits in the 1950s. In addition to
which came the increasing influence and addition of Latin music made
more generally popular in the 1950s and 1960s by Desi Arnaz, Car-
men Miranda, Xavier Cugat, and Pèrez Prado. However, it was Selena,
tragically shot by one of her fans in 1995, who is noted for raising Latin
pop to its previously unprecedented level of popularity. Like Aguilera, Selena began singing as a young child, at age six. Her album *Live!*
won a Grammy (her first) in 1993, and her next album, *Amor Prohibido*
(1994), became the best-selling Latin album of all time. Selena was the
daughter of a Mexican father and an American Mexican mother, and
so, like Aguilera-to-come, she had both cultures influencing her work.
  Gloria Estefan also helped bring Latin pop into the mainstream.
Of Cuban descent, she has won seven Grammys, marking her as extraordinarily successful. Ricky Martin, from Puerto Rico, has won both
Grammy Awards and Latin Grammy Awards and is best known for his
international hit "Livin' La Vida Loca." He has invited Aguilera to
partner with him on some singles, and he is also committed to helping
other Latin pop performers bridge to other genres and markets. With
60 million records sold worldwide, one Grammy Award, one Latin
Grammy Award, and two Billboard Hot 100s, Enrique Iglesias took the

music world by storm thanks to his Mexican label, Fonovisa. Finally, Shakira continues the tradition with a long list of accomplishments, including two Grammy Awards and seven Latin Grammys, making her the top-selling Columbian artist ever. Finally to be mentioned here is Jennifer Lopez, also of Puerto Rican descent, born and raised in the Bronx, and considered to be the wealthiest and most successful of Latin performers with her television and movie roles, music, and all-the-rage perfumes. By some accounts these stars are considered authentic.

Then there are "the others":

> The new wave isn't about fresh, emerging Spanish-language artists; it's about established pop stars co-opting the trappings of Latin mania.[19]

And about Aguilera:

> And bubblegum popster Christina Aguilera putting out a Spanish version of her chart-topper "Genie in a Bottle" called "Genio Atrapado."[20]

Although Aguilera claims credit for pursuing the Spanish version of the single, Bob Jamieson, then president of RCA Records, allegedly pushed her in this direction when he realized she had the ready ticket to enter what he recognized as a new and booming market; that ticket was her Ecuadoran heritage. Of course, there were a few minor complications, not the least of which was the fact that Aguilera needed Spanish lessons. Seeing dollar signs, Jamieson's big concern was whether she would appear credible.

What was Aguilera's response to all of this?

> It's a side that's a part of me. It kind of makes me mad because I hear about a lot of other people who just want to jump on the bandwagon.[21]

Beyond pop came a new genre called "power pop." Power pop is performed on electric guitar, bass, and drums, is no more than three and a half minutes long, has a memory-catching chorus, and is created purely for listening pleasure, not art. An umbrella emerged that united pop and power pop into the Top 40 phenomenon. The concept originates from the jukeboxes of the 1950s, which held 40 singles. The idea sprang from the fact that wherever there were jukeboxes, and wherever there were people, there were songs being played, and some of those songs would inevitably rise to the top. Thus was born the Top 40, which then moved into radio where disc jockeys played those Top 40 songs from jukeboxes across the country. Casey Kasem arrived on the scene in 1970 and heralded the birth of *American Top 40*, where once a week he played the top 40 songs on the Billboard Hot 100 singles chart. In addition to that, he also provided interesting stories and background material involving the songs and their artists. The show became a hit with its weekly countdown format as well as how it drew pop-music lovers from coast-to-coast together.

For many years, radio continued to be the medium for pop music distribution, but that changed in the millennium as technology constantly morphed and widened the available options. This is the field on which Aguilera was to play.

NOTES

1. "Women of Staten Island," *Staten Island Historian*, retrieved December 17, 2009, from http://www.statenislandhistorian.com/Women_of_Staten_Island.html.

2. "Profile for Staten Island," retrieved March 19, 2010, from http://www.epodunk.com/cgi-bin/genInfo.php?locIndex=1751.

3. Ian Urbina, "A Bastion of Black History Amid S.I. Development," *New York Times*, November 4, 2003, retrieved January 1, 2010, from http://www.nytimes.com/2003/11/04/nyregion/they-will-not-be-moved-a-bastion-of-black-history-amid-si-development.html.

4. "Profile for Staten Island."

5. "Lone Star Cultural History, 1980–1989," Lone Star College, retrieved April 2, 2010, from http://kclibrary.lonestar.edu/decade80.html.

6. Ibid.

7. "Men and Women 80's Fashion," Tripletsandus.com, retrieved March 19, 2010, from http://www.tripletsandus.com/80s/fashion.htm.

8. "The American Scene," The Eighties Club, retrieved February 27, 2010, from http://eightiesclub.tripod.com/id44.htm.

9. "The Music Scene," The Eighties Club, retrieved February 26, 2010, from http://eightiesclub.tripod.com/id14.htm.

10. "80's Hits," retrieved March 20, 2010, from http://www.eight yeightynine.com/music/top40.html.

11. Ibid.

12. *New Grove Dictionary of Music and Musicians*, 2nd ed. (New York: Oxford University Press, 2004).

13. David Galenson, "From 'White Christmas' to Sgt. Pepper: The Conceptual Revolution in Popular Music," *Historical Methods* 42, no. 1 (Winter 2009): 19.

14. Ibid.

15. Ibid.

16. Ibid.

17. Robert McChesney, "The Global Media Giants: The Nine Firms That Dominate the World," Fair.org, retrieved February 25, 2010, from http://www.fair.org/extra/9711/gmg.html.

18. Galenson, "From 'White Christmas.'"

19. "Latin Lovers," EW.com, retrieved February 23, 2010, from http://www.ew.com/ew/article/0,,271735,00.html.

20. Ibid.

21. Ibid.

Chapter 3

THE MOUSE THAT ROARED

THE LUCKY RABBIT BECOMES MORTIMER THE MOUSE

Once upon a time there was a bunny rabbit whose name was Oswald the Lucky Rabbit. Oswald was "born" in 1927, to his father and creator, Walt Disney. At the time, Walt owned a small studio called Disney Brothers Studio, which was a small division in the massive enterprise of Universal Pictures. The little studio was charged with creating all the animation for Universal. The long and short of it was that Oswald, complete with huge floppy ears, button nose, and white face, became a huge hit. Success, thought Disney, and thus, with confidence he began negotiations with Universal executives in 1928 for another, and he hoped, more lucrative, contract.

His hope, however, was not to be, and in a shocking move, Universal hired Disney's employees away from him, offered Disney a pittance salary, and took ownership of Oswald. Disney turned down this insulting offer, and so without a job or solid hope, he and one faithful employee, Ub Iwerks, spent many stressful days and nights trying to create Oswald's successor, a character just as unique and popular. And so Oswald's ears were cut off, his middle plumped up, and the lucky rabbit became first, Mortimer Mouse who then morphed to Mickey Mouse, a name, insisted Disney's wife, that was far more suitable than Mortimer.[1]

The evolution of Mickey Mouse, without whom the show of his name would not have existed, was a tale of twists, turns, and tenacity. The first step in the saga was when Mickey became wildly popular after the release of the first cartoon clip, *Steamboat Willie*, which premiered in New York City on November 18, 1928. This film was revolutionary because it was the first cartoon to synchronize sound, music, and action. Thus, *Steamboat Willie* began Disney's journey on the road to remarkable success with animated entertainment products.

Before long, Mickey became a household name, and Disney set off to capitalize on his famous character. Known for his marketing prowess, Disney created and sold various Mickey Mouse memorabilia and merchandise, followed by the introduction of a Mickey Mouse fan club for children, which he dubbed *The Mickey Mouse Club*. The Mickey Mouse character was Disney's bread and butter and so to keep pace with changing audience expectations, he went through several facelifts throughout the 1900s. Then in the years from 1953 to 1983, Disney forayed into new and also profitable ventures such as *Bambi* and *Sleeping Beauty*, sidelining Mickey during those years, except for reruns. But sidelined or not, of one thing there is no doubt, those ears, those unforgettable black ears, are claimed by some to be the most renowned icon of the 20th century.[2]

HISTORY OF THE WALT DISNEY COMPANY

The first feature-length animated film Disney produced was *Snow White and the Seven Dwarfs*, which was met with smashing success and provided him with the money he needed to put down on land in Burbank for another dream: The Walt Disney Studios. Disney, a perfectionist by nature, was involved in every aspect of this venture, even down to the layout of the buildings and design of the animators' chairs.[3]

> His main concern was to produce a self-sufficient, state-of-the-art production factory that provided all the essential facilities for the entire production process.[4]

Disney's early projects at his new studios, produced in the 1940s and 1950s, were more full-length animated films, including *Peter Pan*, *Fantasia*, *Bambi*, *Alice in Wonderland*, and *Cinderella*. Then in the late 1940s he also began to expand into production of live-action feature films and television shows, which he was able to do easily because of the studio's five live-action sound stages. Some of the productions the company became involved with included the television show *Dragnet* and movies *20,000 Leagues under the Sea*, *Mary Poppins*, *Pollyanna*, and *Pirates of the Caribbean* I, II, and III.

Today the company is the second-largest media and entertainment enterprise (behind Time Warner) in the world.[5] In addition to its theme park holdings, the Disney Studios organization distributes movies from a number of other names, including Walt Disney Pictures, Touchstone Pictures, Hollywood Pictures, and Miramax Films. There is also an international distribution arm, a Broadway show production division, several sound track makers, *Disney on Ice*, and many, many more.

A MAN, A DREAM, AND A MAGIC KINGDOM

The next step in the progression toward *The Mickey Mouse Club* was the realization of Disney's dream, born from fodder generated by the adventures of his own daughters. During an outing to a local amusement park when the girls were very young, he noticed how filthy and uncomfortable it was, and how parents had nothing to do but watch their children riding in scummy, dirty rides. And so he dreamed:

> What this country really needs is an amusement park that families can take their children to. They've gotten so honky tonk with a lot of questionable characters running around, and they're not safe. They're not well kept. I want to have a place that's as clean as anything could ever be, and all the people in it are first-class citizens, and treated like guests.[6]

So on July 17, 1955, against formidable, and seemingly unconquerable, odds, Walt Disney's dream came true. This day marked the opening of Disneyland, and for Disney it was a fantasy made real, and the realization of a kingdom that was indeed magical. But opening day did not turn out to be the true fantasy Disney dreamed of. In fact, the day's various foibles resulted in the day being forever known as "Black Sunday."[7] Some of the things that went wrong on that day included the following:

- There was a horrendous, 7-mile-long traffic jam leading to the park.
- Rides broke down throughout the day, of course, while TV crews watched and filmed.
- A gas leak forced closure of one part of the park.
- In some places, fresh asphalt melted and surreptitiously glommed onto the high heels of many women.
- Water fountains throughout the park were not ready in time so annoyed guests went thirsty.

Reviewers pronounced the park too expensive and "poorly managed."[8] But Disney remained undaunted and went on to create one of the world's greatest masterpieces of entertainment:

For those of us who remember the carefree time it recreates, Main Street will bring back happy memories. For younger visitors, it is an adventure in turning back the calendar to the days of grandfather's youth.[9]

However, fast forward to today and the blush of the Disney theme parks has worn off for some in certain camps. Whereas Disney's initial goal was to give parents refuge from the boredom and filth of the standard-variety amusement parks of that time, in reality, some parents and visitors felt his own parks featured the filth and boredom he was trying to escape. As scholar, researcher, and mother to nine children Susan Willis finds, today's park parents look bedraggled and haggard while accompanying their children. She said:

It's an ordeal to go to Disney World. You have to get up very early to get the most out of admission passes, you have to stand in line for hours. Rides, however, have become an almost peripheral attraction. Much of Disney World now is about shopping and probably takes up about 80 percent of the average visitor's time. Some people say our culture is becoming Disney. My questions center around what kind of social realities we develop in an artificial environment based on consumption. What does it mean for our social relationships?[10]

Despite critics, the myriad Disney parks available today flourish and continue to beckon both children and adults who are enchanted by their never-ending magic and fantasy.

HISTORY OF *THE MICKEY MOUSE CLUB*

On the heels of Disney's original and showcase park came another dream, the original *The Mickey Mouse Club*, which first aired in July 1955, a busy time and month indeed for Disney. Besides its namesake animated segments, the core of the program was a group of talented young people. The key to this cast was Disney's belief in hiring "charismatic but ordinary children,"[11] a philosophy that pervaded everything he did.

Annette Funicello, Lisa Whelchel, and more recently, Keri Russell, Ryan Gosling, Justin Timberlake, Britney Spears, and of course, Aguilera: all of these well-known names are alumni of *The Mickey Mouse Club* and have all gone on to enjoy successful entertainment careers.

Funicello was selected by Disney himself when he discovered her at age 12 performing in a local theater production. Although a well-known Mouseketeer, she became even better-known as a result of the series of beach movies in which she starred with Frankie Avalon. Funicello was a Mouseketeer from the beginning of the show in 1955 until its first hiatus in 1959. Funicello has sadly gone on to acquire multiple sclerosis, a disease she kept hidden for many years until her staggered gait and slurred speech set off rumors of alcoholism.

A more recent Mouseketeer, Lisa Whelchel (1977), went on to star in the television series *The Facts of Life*, where she played the snobby yet funny character of Blair Warner.[12] The alumni cast also boasted an impressive award-winning contingency. Keri Russell, a prolific entertainer and actor, emerged from her Mouseketeer days (1991–1993) to star in a multitude of film and television projects. Her most notable accomplishments were the role of Felicity in the hit TV series of the same name (1998–2002), for which she won a Golden Globe

Award. She also starred opposite Tom Cruise in the movie *Mission Impossible III* (2006).[13] Another award-winning actor alumni was Ryan Gosling, Mouseketeer from 1993–1995, who went on to win an Academy Award for his role as Dan Dunne in the movie *Half Nelson* (2006). On the musical side came three Grammy winners including Justin Timberlake (1993–1995), Britney Spears (1993–1995), and Aguilera (1993–1995).

Today, people of all generations have a memory of *The Mickey Mouse Club* in some version unique to the time. In all its versions, *The Mickey Mouse Club* was a variety show for children that featured singing, dancing, and acting performed by ordinary kids with extraordinary talents. The earliest iteration of the show, which aired from 1955–1959, included a newsreel, which was really a 15-minute feature about a person, place, or thing, a cartoon, a story or serial segment featuring the Mouseketeers and guests as characters, and finally, variety segments of dancing, singing, and comedy. *The Mickey Mouse Club* had three "signature" elements with the first being the outfits worn by the cast: pleated skirts for the girls, and nice pants for the boys, both topped by sweaters with the cast member's first name. Second was the roll call of cast members in the beginning of each show, and last was the sign-off song, the words and melody of which echoed in children's dreams.

The magic of *The Mickey Mouse Club* remained deeply embedded in the minds and hearts of the baby boom generation, and so, a revival of the show targeted to their children occurred in January 1977. This was the version in which Lisa Whelchel starred, along with Kelly Parsons who went on to become runner-up in the Miss USA contest. Most of the original format was kept intact with some updating as well as a few minimal changes to lyrics. However, this version was introduced during a time of waning popularity for the Disney Studios and at a time 10 years after Walt's death. The show ended after just one year.

But the magic and memories persisted and the third and final revival occurred in 1989, broadcast on the Disney Channel, a ready-made market for existing young Disney fans. The format of this show was significantly different, with a major update to prequalify it for a fledgling pop audience.[14] Because of its new and hip approach, the show succeeded and ran full course for seven seasons.

THE DIVA ENTERS STAGE RIGHT

In her as yet still blossoming career, one of Aguilera's dreams was to become a member of the famed Mouseketeers of *The New Mickey Mouse Club* television show. However, to become a cast member required auditioning against hundreds and thousands of hopefuls across the nation. Often traveling across country to find hidden stars, the show's producers came to Pittsburgh where 400 anxious children lined up, desperate for one of just several open slots. At just nine years old, Aguilera begged her mother to take her to try out. The audition was daunting. Amazingly, from 400 children, the number of candidates was reduced to six, of which Aguilera was one. However, though she clearly wowed the producers with her talent, the producers ultimately decided she was too young to be a Mouseketeer. Interestingly, two years later, her mother got a phone call one day from a producer of *The New Mickey Mouse Club* who had kept Aguilera's audition tapes on file. Was she available? Was she still interested? Yes, yes, and yes again, said her mother. But, despite the tremendously good sign the phone call suggested, there were still auditions—this time against 15,000 young people from around the country, all of whom were competing for just seven slots.

> Christina Aguilera is going to Disney World. That's where "The Mickey Mouse Club" tapes its shows, and Aguilera, 12, of Rochester, Beaver County, is a new Mouseketeer on the show, which begins its new season Monday on the Disney Channel.[15]

Thus was the text of an item that appeared in Aguilera's local newspaper, a paper that had become well acquainted with the various successes over the years of its very own child prodigy.

A FAMILY AFFAIR

On May 12, 1991, and shortly before Aguilera and her mom took off for Mouseketeering days, Shelly Aguilera became Shelly Kearns when she married James (Jim) Kearns, a paramedic with two children of his own: daughter Stephanie Kearns and son Casey Kearns. Together, they had a son, born April 30, 1996, whom they named Michael James. True to character, Aguilera was wary of her new stepfather for quite some time, but when her guard finally came down, she cared for him deeply, even calling him Dad in both family and professional contexts—as in thanking her "father" when accepting awards.[16]

LIFE IN ORLANDO

For Aguilera, life on the set of *The New Mickey Mouse Club* was idyllic and it wasn't long before she became known as "the Diva" to her fellow cast-mates. She was in her element and at long last, she was among other kids who "understood" and recognized her for who she was. Her contract called for filming a total of 70 episodes of the show, and believe it or not, she had her first-ever dance and voice lessons. Writes Christine Sams of the Sydney, Australia, *Sun Herald*:

> She emerged from the experience with a healthy work ethic and finely tuned onstage technique. And that's not to mention the powerful singing voice, which can still knock socks off her competitors.[17]

Despite being Aguilera's dream come true, between rehearsals, lessons, school work, and filming, life as a Mouseketeer was arduous. Filming took place in Orlando, Florida, from May through the end of October, which required that the families relocate there during that period. Housing was provided in one of the large Disney luxury apartment complexes that had swimming pools, game rooms, laundry facilities, and transportation to the various Disney facilities in Orlando. The families usually all stayed in one complex to facilitate comradeship among the children and their families. During the day, the Mouseketeers were required to study lessons consistent with studies at their home schools for several hours before they went on for the work of the day. But despite the drudgery, she relished the experience that brought her together with like-minded souls. In recalling her Mouseketeer days, Aguilera said:

> The show was like summer camp, all of us coming together. . . . We'd start the school year late and leave school early in the spring.[18]

THE THINGS YOU DON'T HEAR ABOUT

Unfortunately, being a cast member of *The New Mickey Mouse Club* did not guarantee success. Most notably are the trials and heartbreaks of Britney Spears, who went on to experience divorce, wildly impulsive behavior, custody battles, and various addictions that led her in and out of a number of rehabilitation places. The pressure in the biz is relentless and clearly knocks a significant number of prospective young stars and starlets out of the running. But the strong survive, and about that Aguilera has said:

> The pressure is definitely hard, but I think just keeping your head on your shoulders is easier than it looks. I think if you know who you are, then you'll be fine for the rest of the way.[19]

In addition to her extraordinary performing talents, even as a child, Aguilera evidently had the extraordinary ability to center herself and be clear in her mind and soul about her career goals as well as what was important to her on a personal level. These were unusual characteristics for someone so young and would separate her from many of her peers who drowned in the pressures of the entertainment business.

Two years and Aguilera's idyllic life was over. In what must have been a terrible letdown, mother and daughter headed for home where Aguilera never went back to school and was home schooled. This, her mother claimed, was to accommodate Aguilera's continued career growth and burgeoning travel schedule as well as a way to avoid her torment in school.[20]

Waxing philosophical about her Mouseketeer days, Aguilera said:

> It was great preparation for what I'm doing now because of the fact that you had so much on-camera experience every day. And it was really great to be around a lot of other kids who enjoyed performing and were just as passionate and driven about it as you were.[21]

FRIENDS FOR LIFE?

It was during their *The New Mickey Mouse Club* stint that Aguilera and Britney Spears first crossed paths. In fact, not only did they cross paths, they became the best of friends. The youngest cast members, the two girls became inseparable and are said to often have held one another's hands. Also, with their daughters thrown together and their own roles as stage mothers, both Spears's and Aguilera's moms became the best of friends as well. Although minimized in the press, allegedly Aguilera and Spears also did their fair share of fighting during their Mouseketeer days, and supposedly the fighting was over heartthrob Justin Timberlake, who eventually became Spears's boyfriend.[22] But despite real or media-crafted antagonism between the two girls, the fact is that they were two tremendous talents setting the stage for the future of music:

> They were two baby divas who changed the face of pop in the late Nineties, springing from fame on the Disney Channel's New Mickey Mouse Club to the top of the charts in the blink of an eye. Releasing their debut singles within eight months of one another, Christina Aguilera and Britney Spears have been in the spotlight ever since.[23]

The friendship between Aguilera and Spears is rumored to have become volatile after their The New Mickey Mouse Club days as they went their separate ways and nurtured their own careers. In fact, over the years there have been episodes of outright antagonism between the two. Indeed, their careers paralleled, though their closeness succumbed to the pressure cooker of the entertainment world. Into the recording world they plunged with Spears's first hit, "Baby One More Time" coming out eight months before Aguilera's hit, "Genie in a Bottle." "When we both started releasing records, it was a funny time for me," Aguilera said.[24]

However, the real reported trouble between them didn't materialize until 2003 when Aguilera went on the Justified/Stripped tour with Spears's former boyfriend and fellow Mouseketeer Justin Timberlake. One evening after the tour, Spears showed up at Joseph's, a well-known Hollywood hot spot, knowing that both Aguilera and Timberlake would be there and for the express purpose of making up with Aguilera. However, so the story goes, Spears showed up only to find Aguilera and Timberlake embracing. Aguilera insisted it was simply an innocent hug between two close friends. However, no explanation would appease Spears, and so the conflict escalated.

After the hugging incident, Aguilera was working on an album and she discovered that one of the songs was written by someone named Aurora Lynne, which turned out to be a pseudonym for Spears. When Aguilera discovered that Spears had written it, that was the end of that song on that album.

The next incident occurred when Aguilera was asked by the press to comment on Spears's engagement to Kevin Federline. Her response was less than complimentary, and she referred to Federline as "low rent."[25] No reported response from Spears emerged, but it is fairly certain that Aguilera's comment did not set well. In fact, after the incident, Aguilera wrote a letter to Spears hoping they could resolve things and become friends once more. Spears never responded.

"There have been many stories about the two of us not getting on. . . . We don't keep closely in touch with one another, and it's obvious how our lives have taken on two different directions,"[26] said Aguilera.

Have they really taken on different directions? In some ways yes, most notably, Aguilera's seemingly stable and focused personal and professional lives. When Spears had her first child in 2005, Aguilera sent her a basket filled with presents, and once more, received no reply. When asked about Spears's many personal troubles, Aguilera responded by saying, "I don't pass any judgment on what she does. . . . I wish her all the best."[27]

AT WHAT PRICE LOLITA?

As glorious as it may seem, the toll on young performers can be heavy. Not only are their careers often vaporized after successful runs as child stars, but there is also the issue of what young children dressed as sexy vamps does to not only the child, but society in general.

Aguilera has clearly segued from childhood to adult success with seeming ease, except for the mocking and taunting she faced by classmates. Others who have emerged from childhood stardom to adult renown include movie director/producer Ron Howard and actor/producer/director Jodie Foster. But many more have faded silently into the sunset, facing rates of drug and alcohol abuse three times that of average.[28] Take Paul Petersen, probably the Mouseketeer with the shortest Disney duration. At age nine, when after three weeks of increasing stress because of being mocked, jeered, and called "mouse" because of his small stature, he hauled off and punched the casting head in the stomach. "I was fired for conduct unbecoming a mouse," Petersen said.[29] After winning his battle with drugs following his career crash, he went on to become an activist for the rights and protection of child actors, having founded "A Minor Consideration," a group that provides training and seminars for parents of young performers, offers counseling services for all members, and lobbies for legislation to provide safe work environments for children in entertainment.

Another issue with child performers is their portrayals as young Lolitas and Casanovas, a role Aguilera embraced in her teens. But she is not alone. Some of her predecessors included Brooke Shields who became intrinsically close to her Calvins, as in jeans. Shields was just 15 when those ads hit the airwaves and stunned television audiences. "The 'new and different' ingredient seems to be a provocativeness in ads that depict couples discoing and cavorting in suggestive proximity while the camera dwells on the contour of their jeans."[30] But then there is the tragic example of JonBenet Ramsey, the six-year-old beauty pageant princess who was found murdered in the basement of her parents' home in Colorado. "Television ran footage of the 6-year-old's lipsticked smile when she lowered the strap of her gown to give a glimpse of her shoulder in an inspired imitation of a burlesque dancer."[31]

As we will see in later chapters, Aguilera relished her sexuality. To her it represented the freedom to express herself. But to others, it's seen as dangerously provocative. Debra Merskin of the University of Oregon examined media images of Lolita and wrote:

> It is important to note that depictions of child sexual abuse showed the child unharmed or having benefited from the activity. In 2001, Dark-art directed a *Rolling Stone* cover featuring Christina Aguilera with shorts unzipped and her "athletic tongue licking her lascivious lips."[32]

Whatever the price for the young Aguilera, it has been kept quiet and discreet. As well, there could be no price at all as the young girl

with the big ears went on to become the beautiful young woman with
the red lips.

NOTES

1. Claire Suddath, "Mickey Mouse," Time.com, retrieved December 25, 2009, from http://www.time.com/time/arts/article/0,8599,1859 935,00.html.

2. Ibid.

3. "The Walt Disney Studios History," Walt Disney studios, retrieved February 27, 2010, from http://studioservices.go.com/disney studios/history.html.

4. Ibid.

5. "The Walt Disney Company: Company Description," Hoovers. com, retrieved February 27, 2010, from http://www.hoovers.com/com pany/The_Walt_Disney_Company/rrjfyi-1.html.

6. "Walt Disney's Disneyland," Just Disney.com, retrieved December 25, 2009, from http://www.justdisney.com/walt_disney/biography/ w_disneyland.html.

7. Betsy Malloy, "The Dream: Early Disneyland History," About. com, retrieved December 25, 2009, from http://gocalifornia.about.com/ od/cadisneyland/a/history.htm.

8. "Disneyland's History," Just Disney.com, retrieved December 25, 2009, from http://www.justdisney.com/disneyland/history.html.

9. Ibid.

10. William Sasser, "Inside the Mouse: Deconstructing Disney," *Perspectives*, retrieved February 28, 2010, from http://www.dukemaga zine.duke.edu/alumni/dm1/inmouse.txt.html.

11. http://www.ultimatedisney.com/mickeymouseclub-britneyjustin christina.html.

12. "The Facts of Life," Imdb.com, retrieved July 6, 2010, from http://www.imdb.com/title/tt0078610/.

13. "Keri Russell," Imdb.com, retrieved July 6, 2010, from http://www.imdb.com/name/nm0005392/.

14. http://www.ultimatedisney.com/mickeymouseclub-britneyjustin christina.html.

15. "A Beaver County Mouseketeer," *Pittsburgh Post-Gazette*, October 2, 1993.

16. "Family," retrieved March 23, 2010, from http://www.xtina-web.com/family.php.

17. Christine Sams, "The Mouse That Roared," *Sun Herald* (Sydney, Australia), July 22, 2007.

18. Richard Harrington, "Christina Aguilera's Fast Track: Ex-Mouseketeer Has the Voice to Pull Away from Teen Pop Pack," *Washington Post*, February 13, 2000.

19. Emma Cowing, "The Mouse Trap," *Scotsman*, April 8, 2008.

20. Pier Dominguez, *Christina Aguilera: A Star Is Made* (Phoenix: Colossus Books, 2003).

21. Ed Masley, "Blessed by a 'Genie,'" *Pittsburgh Post-Gazette*, August 13, 1999.

22. "Christina Aguilera," Celebspin.com, retrieved July 6, 2010, from http://www.celebspin.com/2006/07/christina-aguilera/.

23. Adrian Thrills, "Britney? I Wish Her All the Best . . . Honest!," *Daily Mail* (London), November 7, 2008, retrieved October 30, 2009, from http://www.dailymail.co.uk/tvshowbiz/article-1083708/Britney-I-wish-best--honest-Christina-Aguilera-calls-time-pops-bitterest-feuds.html, para 1.

24. Ibid., para 4.

25. Ibid., para 11.

26. Ibid., para 13.

27. Ibid., para 15.

28. Ralph Blumenthal, "A Guiding Hand for Child Actors: Former Stars Seek More Safeguards for Present Ones," *New York Times*, September 2, 1997, retrieved August 30, 2009, from http://www.nytimes.com/1997/09/02/movies/former-stars-seek-more-safeguards-for-present-ones.html?pagewanted=1?pagewanted=1.

29. Ibid., para 4.

30. Christopher Swan, "Advertising and the Lolita Image," *Christian Science Monitor*, February 5, 1981, retrieved September 24, 2009, from http://www.csmonitor.com/1981/0205/020559.html, para 43.

31. Lorrayne Anthony, "Innocents and Experience: Images of Sexy Children Aren't Just the Domain of Pedophiles and Pornographers," *Gazette* (Montreal, Quebec), January 27, 2003.

32. Debra Merskin, "Reviving Lolita?," *American Behavioral Scientist* 48, no. 1 (September 2004): 121–122, retrieved May 2, 2009, from http://www.ac.wwu.edu/~karlberg/444/readings/lolita.pdf.

Chapter 4

BECOMING GOOD CHRISTINA

If there was ever a mouse that roared, Aguilera is a woman who embodies the success of adults making the transition from child stardom.[1]

The events from Aguilera's Mouseketeer days and ending with the release of her first album are a bit sketchy, presumably because of deals gone awry and subsequent legal battles. But the sketch of the story goes something like this: when she was just 12 and still in her *The New Mickey Mouse Club* days, it is purported that public relations expert Ruth Inniss was visiting the studios one day, heard Aguilera sing, and immediately went to find Aguilera's mother. Inniss was, to say the least, impressed, and arranged to stay in touch with Aguilera and her mother until Aguilera's contract with Disney was over. Then in 1994, Kearns agreed that Inniss would become Aguilera's manager when Aguilera's first record deal was signed. In order to do right by her talented young protégée, Inniss supposedly met with a well-respected and experienced talent management group, Dartmouth Management Company, headed by lawyer Normand Kurtz and his executive son, Steven. At some point after this, the two Kurtzes, both of whom were well acquainted with her talent, evidently steered Aguilera and Kearns away from Inniss with the signing of a management contract between them and Aguilera in 1995. Since Aguilera did not as yet have her first record deal, as per Aguilera's mother's agreement with Inniss, there was no contract. Subsequently, Inniss filed a $7 million lawsuit against both Kearns and Steven Kurtz, which probably explains the mystery surrounding details leading to Aguilera's first album.

In the midst of these dealings, Aguilera was frustrated that a record deal was not forthcoming and so in 1997, she traveled to Japan to jump-start her career. While there she performed and recorded the Sheryl Crow song "All I Wanna Do" in duet with popular Japanese singer Keizo Nakanishi. The recording and performances were well received. She also traveled to Brasov, Romania, where she performed to less than enthusiastic crowds as the U.S. representative in the prestigious Golden Stag Festival singing competition. Her mediocre reception was mainly due to her newcomer status as a performer and the fact that she was competing against the likes of Sheryl Crow and Diana Ross.

The Golden Stag Festival is an international pop music fest originally formed to recognize greatness in the genre. First held in 1968, over the years the festival has hosted such notables as James Brown, Ricky Martin, Kenny Rogers, Pink, as well as been the debut venue for many, including Julio Iglesias. The history of the festival parallels the politics of Europe during its era, covering 30 plus years, not all of which were festival years. The idea for a music festival in Romania came from then dictator of the country Nicolae Ceausescu, who wanted the rest of the world to see that Romania was free, that it was no longer under Russian rule. And so, organizers put together this unusual event where:

> The most important thing is that all competitors and their musical managers should understand and "feel" the idea of an International Music Festival. They should have a sincere passion for music and exuberance [sic].[2]

In other words, said festival organizers, it should be "a competition involving the spirit."[3]

After 1971, Ceausescu put an end to the still-fledgling festival because, ironically, he feared the Romanian people would become too exposed to freedom and that might threaten his rule. Finally, it was revived again in 1992. In one of her earliest interviews, then 16-year-old Aguilera was queried by the Romanian press about both her life and her music. Even at that age, Aguilera answered the questions with an unabashed and clear focus about her career, her study of famous artists for technique, and the development of a style all her own. When asked, or rather, told, that her life was easy, Aguilera calmly corrected the interviewer and explained that to become a true star meant to work hard and eat meals away from the security of home. And when asked about her private life, she curtly replied, "It will remain private." Her performance for the festival included the duet of "All I Wanna Do," with Keizo Nakanishi of Japan, and her own set—a song by Sheryl Crow and another by Diana Ross.[4]

AND SO IT BEGAN

Then, in 1998 things began to get interesting for Aguilera.

Producers for an upcoming Disney movie, *Mulan*, were looking for someone who could sing high E above middle C, which to most people's amazement, not only could Aguilera do exquisitely, but she could also do a cappella. Her manager Kurtz sent over to the Disney Studios a tape of Aguilera singing Whitney Houston's "I Wanna Run to You" that she made in her living room using just a boom box. Aguilera didn't think she would get the job, but not only did she get it, she was in the studio in a day's time to make the recording of what became the hit single "Reflection."

Mulan premiered in June 1998, and soon after, "Reflection" turned into a Top 15 hit on the Adult Contemporary singles charts. Aguilera quickly gained additional exposure when she sang "Reflection" on the CBS *This Morning* show as well as on *The Donnie and Marie Show*. Eventually the song garnered a Golden Globe Nomination for Best Original Song in a Motion Picture.

Ron Fair turned out to be Aguilera's fair-haired angel as the executive from RCA Records who heard her sing toward the end of her *The New Mickey Mouse Club* days and kept her, and her astonishing voice, in the back of his mind. Despite the issues with Inniss, the deal was made in 1998 and about her artistry, Fair said:

She is a badass genius of singing. She was put on this earth to sing, and I've worked with a lot of singers. . . . When Aguilera met with us, she didn't care that she was auditioning for a record deal; she got into a performance zone that you see in artists much more mature than she is.[5]

Amazingly, it was during the same week she recorded "Reflection" that she also signed the record contract with RCA Records. Fair, who was then senior vice-president, and the man who found and signed Aguilera, was a record company executive who had worked with the best of the best. About Aguilera he said: "She's got the pipes to be the next Barbra Streisand or Celine Dion, and that, to us, is really all that matters."[6]

So for the next year, from 1998–1999, the record company made Aguilera a project that included voice lessons, wardrobe and makeup coaching, as well as making sure she was seen in the right places with the right people. Aguilera relished the fuss, especially the instructions on how to protect her most valuable tool—her voice. As for the nitty-gritty, RCA hired songwriting heavy hitters Diane Warren, Carl Strunken, and David Frank, and all of this when she was an innocent, sweet 17.

Though Fair called her a "world class talent,"[7] he also knew that Aguilera had not as yet defined herself through her singing style, and this was the primary reason it took so long for her first album to finally be released. He wanted to make sure they had just the right songs done just the right way. Fair said:

She was very much a raw talent, so building a collection of songs that would become her first album was a time-consuming process. We wanted to find the ones that would knock the door down and put her up there.[8]

THE BUSY GENIE

Almost reaching her goal of launching her first album before she finished her schooling, on August 24, 1999, *Christina Aguilera* was released. Within the first month of its release, it reached the top of Billboard 200 and sold 8 million albums in the United States.[9]

Aptly named, it was the single "Genie in a Bottle" that really launched Aguilera to the heights of stardom. For five weeks, "Genie" conquered the Billboard singles chart. It also had a long run on MTV's teen-based *Total Request Live* television show. Then "What a Girl Wants" became the first No. 1 single on Billboard's Hot 100 in the new millennium, a major factor in pushing the album to become Platinum repeatedly. A third song, "Come on over Baby," became the third single from the album to hit No. 1—later in 2000. "Genie in a Bottle," "What a Girl Wants," and "Come on over Baby (All I Want Is You)" all hit the top of Billboard's Hot 100 in 1999 and 2000, and "I Turn to You" was on the Top 5 in the United States, and she won a Grammy Award for Best New Artist for 2000.[10]

In producing the album, the writers and producers worked with her to showcase her talent with each song. Veteran songwriter Steve Kipner (co-wrote "Genie in a Bottle") was impressed with her because she could improvise, and "she did not need coaching to improvise complex R&B lines, a skill he says he generally sees only in older artists."[11]

The album track consisted of:

"Genie in a Bottle"	3:39
"What a Girl Wants"	3:35
"I Turn to You"	4:33
"So Emotional"	4:00
"Come on over Baby (All I Want Is You)"	3:09
"Reflection"	3:33
"Love for All Seasons"	3:59
"Somebody's Somebody"	5:03
"When You Put Your Hands on Me"	3:35
"Blessed"	3:05
"Love Will Find a Way"	3:56
"Obvious"	3:58

But all was not golden. Despite fantastic general acclaim, *Rolling Stone's* review of Aguilera's album was less than enthusiastic. Said Barry Walters with a dose of sarcasm: "Is there room on the pop charts for one more ex-Mouseketeer?" After considerable criticism of her music, he praised her as an "eighteen-year-old bombshell whose greatest assets are her powerhouse pipes."[12]

On the other hand, based on the charts, with "Genie" Aguilera came exploding out of the bottle, tantalizing fans with a haunting mixture of little-girl innocence and vampy sensuality.

> Aguilera is on to something here, an image of bottled-up female sexuality that preys upon age-old fantasies of danger, power and really cool scarves. And somehow, the fact that Aguilera would undoubtedly be singing DIANE WARREN ballads gives "Genie in a Bottle" even more of a sinister kick.[13]

This first in a long line of Aguilera's hit records did not require the full spectrum of her vocal range, though it did begin her evolution to the sexy, sultry side of herself.

Her best to date, 1999 was a knockout year for Aguilera. On the heels of her musical success came notoriety in other ways: in 1999, *Ladies' Home Journal* named her among the magazine's most fascinating women of the year. Recognition of her Hispanic background was evident in being given the 1999 Best New Artists ALMA award, an organization that honors members of the Hispanic American community. In addition, she graced the following magazine covers: *Entertainment Weekly*, *Teen People*, and *Latina*; she was a guest on *Saturday Night Live*, *The Tonight Show* with Jay Leno, *The Rosie O'Donnell Show*, and she was the only female guest on VH1 *Men Strike Back*.

Then there were the television specials: *The Essence Awards*, *Disney Summer Jams*, *People Magazine's 25 Hottest Stars under 25*; she performed a critically acclaimed duet with B. B. King, and she also performed for then President Clinton in a Christmas television special: *Christmas at the White House*. Clinton was so dazzled by Aguilera's performance that he also asked her to sing the first song of the New Year during his television special for the millennium. Aguilera had to turn Clinton down, however, as she had already signed on for the New Year's Eve in Times Square special with Carson Daly, famous host of MTV's hit *Total Request Live* television show.

Indeed, the currents that carried Aguilera to success had become raging rapids.

AGUILERA'S IDOLS

As already mentioned, for Aguilera, it all began in her bedroom, when, night after night, she sought refuge with Julie Andrews and *The Sound of Music*. She played this recording over and over, singing at the top of her lungs, pretending that she was her childhood idol, Julie Andrews. Though she never lost her admiration for Andrews, her idol repertoire later grew to include Whitney Houston, Billie Holiday, and Etta James. James emerged to the top of her list, and about her Aguilera said:

> She's what I want to be someday: sitting on a stool in some smoky jazz club, doing bluesy versions of my old hits like "What a Girl Wants" with just a piano—I'll still be as raunchy as I wanna be and I'll have the memory of Etta James to back me up. It's funny: Etta told me she had heard I was "a little hotheaded," and you know what she said? "Just like me—a girl after my own heart!" I love her feisty vibe.[14]

To her complete thrill, James and Aguilera were engaged in a mutual admiration society. About Aguilera, James said:

> I've always been a complainer—that's what I liked about her. She reminds me of myself when I was young. The bad-girl syndrome was a controversy then, but that was also the hip thing. Everybody wanted to be the bad girl! She has this fabulous little figure but a heavy, almost operatic voice. When she opens her mouth I can hear Billie Holiday and Dinah Washington. She's an old soul.[15]

SWEET, YOUNG, AND NAÏVE

In a scene reminiscent of the play *Annie*, when Annie first arrived at Daddy Warbuck's mansion and was overwhelmed by being dressed and primped, Aguilera's early photo shoots were rife with hairdressers, makeup artists, and manicurists hovering over her while speaking about her in the third person.

"Do you like her hair like this?" a hairdresser asked.
  "Do you think she looks too yellow?" a makeup artist asked.
  "Shouldn't we change her nail polish?" a manicurist asked.[16]

As these and two dozen other people fluttered about, answering cell phones, eating patè and drinking champagne, the diminutive Aguilera curled more and more tightly into herself and looked at times as if she might actually suck her thumb. Although known for her confidence throughout childhood, this was a whole different milieu, this was the big time! Also, as she has often said, on stage she is totally sure and confident, offstage she is shy and quite retiring. Even so, when her manager got a call to book her on *The Tonight Show*, and in her sweet young naïvety, she asked him what show it is.

FOOD, GLORIOUS FOOD

Although a predilection for fast food is not necessarily an indicator of age, it certainly can be a sign of youth. Aguilera was a fast food fanatic. McDonald's? Burger King? KFC? Wendy's? Which of these fast food favorites was the Diva's choice delicacy? Delicacy—not quite, but the stories go that Aguilera lusted over Wendy's; however, in a pinch, McDonald's would do.

Here's how serious her cravings can be:

One evening, while being chauffeured to her Upper West Side apartment in Manhattan, the craving hit. She directs the driver to find a Mickey D's. The driver navigates the stretch around the curves of the drive-through and stops when the singer's window is next to the speaker. She orders a five-piece McNugget meal with hot mustard sauce and a supersize Coke. The staff, all Aguilera's age and younger, climb over each other at the pickup window like a pile of curious ferrets to peer into the dark car.[17]

In spite of her love for fast food, and any food, for that matter, Aguilera's youth and energy allowed her to burn off whatever calories she consumed. And unlike many of her peers, she did not engage in never-ending diets and constant exercise. Aguilera enjoyed her soda pops, hamburgers, French fries, donuts, and reams of junk food, ever claiming how she simply loved to eat. And, of course, exercise was not a word in her vocabulary. She was therefore proud of her svelte self and took great pride in showing off her body. In fact, it has even been said that she has the most recognizable belly button in history. As she slid toward her older teen years, her fashion trademark became her belly, complete with its associated decorations. It was later written:

> The 19-year-old hotshot chanteuse behind "What a Girl Wants," once a Mouseketeer alongside Britney Spears, can't quite pull off pop star flash without belly flopping.[18]

Of course, her belly has been fodder for many discussions along the way. Some are all for its sexy allure; others are less enthusiastic: "Aguilera was a little girl lost in a tummy-baring fringed tee and flowing skirt."[19]

HER HISPANIC HERITAGE

Aguilera was never defined as strictly Latino as in the cases of Ricky Martin, Jennifer Lopez, and Enrique Iglesias. But according to Ron Fair, although she did indeed represent regular American teens who just happened to be of Latin descent, it was her talent and voice that mattered, not her cultural background.[20]

However, when the Latin trend became popular, Aguilera joined the fray with her Spanish recording of "Genie in a Bottle," titled "Genio Atrapado" in Spanish. The recording was an immediate success and resulted in her becoming a "rare cross-over success from the pop mainstream to the Latino market."[21] Then, in September 2000, and marking the beginning of the emergence of the real Aguilera, her album Mi Reflejo, which was designed to celebrate her Latin heritage, was released. "I've always been proud of my Ecuadoran heritage. Recording a Spanish album and working with a great producer like Rudy Perez, gave me a chance to explore my Latin side."[22] This album, which contained a mixture of Spanish translations of her English releases as well as new Spanish songs, led her to a Latin Grammy (2001) for Best Female Pop Vocal Album, sales of 2.1 million copies worldwide, including achieving certified Gold status in the United States (500,000) and 3x Platinum for (600,000 Latin album) RIAA Premios de Oro y Platino program.[23] It also reached No. 27 on the Billboard 200. One of the album's singles, "Falsas Esperanzas" achieved Top 40 status in Argentina. As a result of her Latino success, Martin asked her to sing a duet "Nobody Wants to Be Lonely" on his album *Sound Loaded*. The single reached No. 5 in both the United Kingdom and Germany, Top 20 in the United States, and the Top 40 in Canada, Switzerland, and Australia.

Aguilera's choice of Perez was about as sure a thing as possible for a new album in a new market for an existing superstar. He has been extraordinarily successful as both songwriter and music producer with an astounding 600 songs for the likes of Julio Iglesias, Michael Bolton, Luis Miguel, Luis Fonsi, Marc Anthony, and of course, Aguilera, under his belt. The proof of his success lies in his many gold and platinum records as well as the 15 Grammy Award nominations, of which he won five. Like Aguilera, Perez is also a Disney alumnus, but in the role of songwriter/producer for the song "Colors of the Wind" from the animated film *Pocahontas*. Perez credits his career to his discovery by, and 20-year professional association and friendship with, Jose Feliciano.

Soon after recording her Spanish album *Mi Reflejo*, Aguilera recorded her Christmas album, *My Kind of Christmas*, where her singing was supported by a 70-piece orchestra. The album included new tracks, traditional tracks, and a duet with Dr. John singing "Merry Christmas Baby," and climbed to No. 28 on the Billboard 200, became certified Platinum, and sold a total of 1.3 million albums.

The icing on the cake of another amazingly successful year (2001) for Aguilera was an All Star Tribute remake of Marvin Gaye's "What's Going On" which, in addition to Aguilera, involved many stars including Bono and Nelly Furtado.

SLIM SHADY WON'T SIT DOWN

To get in the minds, hearts, and souls of the teen pop, and tremendously lucrative, audience was to get your song played on MTV's popular show *Total Request Live (TRL)*, hosted by Carson Daly. "Genie" had a long and successful run on *TRL*, which helped make it a hit. The show ran for 10 years, broadcast live on weekday afternoons from its glass-enclosed Times Square studio. Young people gathered outside to see their favorite stars, screaming all the way, their cacophony a barometer to their favorite stars' popularity. In the meantime, fans at home watching on television would vote for their favorite songs and artists by phone.

At the time, there were rampant rumors about Aguilera's love life: "You can be 19 and be drop dead cute and still be out of synch with the tides of youthful romance when you're on a never-ending promotional mission."[24] A self-espoused addict of gossip magazines, she delighted in keeping up with her own "romances" with the likes of Daly, Eminem, and scores more. In fact, the lady herself has been known to "squeeze her own juice": "If I can't really date, at least I can think about it, or think about having crushes. It's just fun, and they never last very long, my crushes."[25]

But things got carried away with her alleged romance with Daly and soon she was rumored to have been involved with him in various sexual exploits. In fact, hip-hop singer Eminem claimed that Aguilera performed oral sex on Daly, as well as Fred Durst, a member of the band Limp Bizkit. And so, in his song, "The Real Slim Shady," Eminem parodied these exploits of Aguilera's, as well as took hits on other stars including actress Pamela Anderson, comedian Tom Green, rapper Will Smith, and Aguilera's nemesis, Britney Spears.

Aguilera's comment was: "It's disgusting and offensive and above all it's not true."[26]

Aguilera and Eminem eventually made peace, at the 2002 MTV award ceremony where Aguilera actually presented him with an award. After a few words of explanation the two ended up in a hug. On the other hand and what would become ironic later on, singer Kelly Osbourne, daughter of heavy metal singer Ozzy Osbourne, was not quite so generous about Aguilera: "She's one of the most disgusting human beings in the world, is Christina Aguilera [sic]. She's despicable for so many reasons."[27]

A parody of the song, "Will the Real Slim Shady Please Shut Up" showed up on the airwaves before long, and many mistakenly thought it was sung by Aguilera. It was actually performed by rapper Emily Ellis for the radio station KLUC in Las Vegas, Nevada, but quickly exploded to a nationwide hit of its own accord.

In many camps, rumors indeed flew about Aguilera and Daly, but the truth remained couched in secrecy. But one thing did not remain secret and that was that Daly became a national heartthrob as a result of his *TLR* gig, eliciting screams from fans wherever he went. He was a golfer, having once caddied for O. J. Simpson, and even won a golf scholarship to Loyola Marymount University in Los Angeles. He decided college wasn't for him after just one year and dropped out to take an internship at a radio station, which was the launching pad for his career. Daly got air time during his internship, which led to disc jockey jobs after, which directly then led to his job as host on MTV.[28]

THE MAGIC MOMENT

It was February 2000 and Aguilera unquestionably soared to the height of heights when the grand diva team of Melissa Etheridge, Sheryl Crow, and Sara McLaughlan announced and awarded her the Grammy for Best New Artist. Bursting from her seat in an emotional moment of shock, Aguilera ran to the stage, dressed in a gorgeous, shimmery-silvery short dress, hands over her mouth to accept the award and thank, among professional others, her "Mom," and "Dad," referring to her stepfather, Jim Kearns, and not her real father, Xavier Aguilera.

About that admittedly stunned moment, Aguilera said:

> It was an incredible shock for me. . . . I was completely unprepared. My album had been out the least amount of time compared to everyone else, so I thought there was no way I'd win. But I was overwhelmed, shocked and overjoyed all at the same time.[29]

Aguilera was truly flabbergasted by her win because at the time, she only had the hit single "Genie in a Bottle." As well, she was competing against Britney Spears whose single had been out a good eight months before Aguilera's. But this was only the beginning.

BUBBLEGUM IS STICKY

Life continued to be interesting for Aguilera in 2000 as her popularity as the pop bubblegum princess soared. However, she wasn't soaring with it. Her manager at that time, Steve Kurtz, was apparently driving her into the ground with a grueling, nonstop schedule that contributed to her contracting a series of viral and throat infections. Kurtz also pressured her to keep her cash-cow, bubblegum princess image. But Aguilera wasn't so much interested in reeling in the money as she was developing her art as a singer and performer. In a move to shed what she felt was a stifling image that did not represent her true self, she filed suit against Kurtz for "improper, undue, and inappropriate influence over her professional activities as well as fraud."[30]

During the course of this legal action, Aguilera also discovered that Kurtz was taking more than his agreed-upon commission allegedly for hiring assistants, a move that was not approved by Aguilera. The deal she had made with him was that any additional assistance would come out of his 20-percent commission. In sum, her claim was that Kurtz was in it strictly for Kurtz, not for Aguilera. Fortunately for Aguilera, her contract with Kurtz was deemed null and void by the California State Labor Commission. When the matter with Kurtz was settled, she hired Irving Azoff as her new manager, a notably tough contender when it came to protecting his clients and who refused to overbook them. His aggressive personality did not endear him to many in the business, but his style worked for Aguilera and opened the door for her to pursue her startlingly sensuous, and some said raunchy, image.

NOTES

1. Christine Sams, "The Mouse That Roared," *Sun Herald* (Sydney, Australia), July 22, 2007, retrieved July 25, 2009, from http://www.smh.com.au/news/people/the-mouse-that-roared/2007/07/22/1185042926582.html, para 13.

2. "The Golden Stag Festival History," Brazov Travel Guide, n.d., retrieved March 23, 2010, from http://www.brasovtravelguide.ro/en/brasov/events/golden-stag-festival/index.php.

3. Ibid.

4. "The Tenth Edition of the Golden Stag Festival," Brazov Travel Guide, n.d., retrieved March 23, 2010, from http://www.brasovtravelguide.ro/en/brasov/events/golden-stag-festival/index.php.

5. Anthony Bozza, "The Christina Aguilera Story (so far)," *Rolling Stone*, October 28, 1999.

6. Alisa Valdes-Rodriguez, "Genie behind Bottle," *Los Angeles Times*, July 26, 1999, retrieved August 26, 2009, from http://articles.latimes.com/1999/jul/26/entertainment/ca-59618?pg=1, para 36.

7. Richard Harrington, "Christina Aguilera's Fast Track: Ex-Mouseketeer Has the Voice to Pull Away from Teen Pop Pack," *Washington Post*, February 13, 2000, LexisNexis, 2.

8. Ibid., 2.

9. "Christina Aguilera," 8notes.com, retrieved July 6, 2010, from http://www.8notes.com/biographies/aguilera.asp.

10. Ibid.

11. Valdes-Rodriguez, "Genie behind Bottle."

12. *Christina Aguilera* album review, Barry Walters, retrieved October 5, 2009, from http://www.rollingstone.com/reviews/album/207283/review/5941389?utm_source=Rhapsody&utm_medium=CDreview.

13. Rob Sheffield, "Christina Aguilera's Bottle Rocket," *Rolling Stone*, August 19, 1999.

14. Christina News Source, http://www.christinamultimedia.com/newssource/.

15. Ibid.

16. Valdes-Rodriguez, "Genie behind Bottle."

17. Bozza, "The Christina Aguilera Story," *Rolling Stone*, October 28, 1999.

18. "Christina Aguilera," *People*, September 18, 2000.

19. Ibid., para 1.

20. Valdes-Rodriguez, "Genie behind Bottle."

21. "Hispanic Heritage: Christina Aguilera," Gale Cengage Learning, n.d., retrieved August 8, 2009, from http://www.gale.cengage.com/free_resources/chh/bio/aguilera_c.htm.

22. "Christina Aguilera Biography," Sing365.com, retrieved July 6, 2010, from http://www.sing365.com/music/lyric.nsf/Christina-Aguilera-Biography/30A2CB1B87B22F2B482568660008B07E.

23. "Biography," Christina Aguilera's Site, Simplyaguilera.com/biography.html.

24. Harrington, "Christina Aguilera's Fast Track," LexisNexis, 3.

25. Ibid., 3.

26. Ibid., 2.

27. "Kiss and Make Up," *Herald Sun* (Melbourne, Australia), November 28, 2002.

28. "Carson Daly Biography," Imdb.com, retrieved March 5, 2010, from http://www.imdb.com/name/nm0004856/bio.

29. "Christina Aguilera Biography," Sing365.com, http://www.sing365.com/music/lyric.nsf/Christina-Aguilera-Biography/30A2CB1B87B22F2B482568660008B07E.

30. "Christina Aguilera," Celebspin.com, retrieved July 6, 2010, from http://www.celebspin.com/2006/07/christina-aguilera/.

Chapter 5

BECOMING BAD X-TINA

Aguilera desperately wanted to shed the cute little Aguilera, good girl image that her first album, *Christina Aguilera*, was all about. She wanted to do her own thing, experiment with both her identity and her art. This meant becoming free. This meant firing her then manager Kurtz and hiring a new manager, Azoff, the first steps in her journey to a darker image. Another step in this self-evolutionary process was taking artistic control for her career, a move she made evident in her role in "Lady Marmalade."

"LADY MARMALADE" AND *MOULIN ROUGE*

The tide indeed continued to create great waves for Aguilera. Her next project was the 2001 hit song "Lady Marmalade" from the motion picture *Moulin Rouge*, in which she starred along with Pink, Mýa, and Lil' Kim. The original version of "Lady Marmalade" was released in 1974 by an all-female group, Labelle, and as it was for Aguilera and company, the song was a megahit. In fact, it was voted into the Grammy Hall of Fame in 2003. More sensational in 1974 than 2001, however, was the song's trademark: the suggestive and racy chorus: "Voulez-vous coucher avec moi (ce soir)?," which means "Do you want to sleep with me (to-night)?" The song was originally written by Bob Crew, and Aguilera's version was produced by Missy Elliott.

An interesting fact is that the sensational "Lady Marmalade" video, directed by Paul Hunter, was not shot with all four women at the same time, yet when all four recordings were synched together, the effect was seamless and stunning. All four were sexily dressed in lingerie on a set in Los Angeles designed to look like the inside of the actual Moulin Rouge nightclub in Paris. This smash hit spent five weeks in the No. 1 slot of the Billboard Hot 100 and was named MTV Best Video of the Year for 2001. It was also No. 1 in 11 other countries. In addition, in 2002, each "Lady" won a Grammy for Best Pop Collaboration with Vocals.

So thanks to "Lady Marmalade," Aguilera continued her winning pole vault into the music scene, a diminutive 5'2", platinum blonde, sexy red lips, with a "skilled soprano voice that has catapulted her into the modern pantheon of diva stardom."[1] Her voice and talent was compared to the best of the best, and Celine Dion called her the best female singer in the world today.[2] "She is," wrote Elizabeth Day, "re-

Christina Aguilera sings "Lady Marmalade" from the film Moulin Rouge, *at the 2001 MTV Movie Awards in Los Angeles, June 2, 2001. AP Photo/Mark J. Terrill.*

freshingly dismissive. . . . Instead, she is almost absurdly matter-of-fact about it."[3] Absurd indeed, when at the time she was asked about her vocal range, she admitted that she did not know the expanse of her full range. Her blasé attitude was indeed evidence of a young woman who was seemingly not impressed with herself as many divas can be. On the other hand, perhaps success was exploding around her so much that the range of her voice just didn't mean anything anymore.

However, despite its smashing success, there was also criticism for her sexy, suggestive performance in "Lady Marmalade." It didn't seem to bother Aguilera, however. She said:

> Everybody said "Don't do 'Lady Marmalade,' it's too urban for you!" But I wanted to do it. The girls [Pink, Lil' Kim, Mýa, and Missy Elliott] were great to work with—it was like, "Let's play dress-up for a day!" If you're doing a video for a movie like *Moulin Rouge*—I mean, it's about a whorehouse—you have to get up there in some fun costumes. I love taking chances.[4]

But this was only the beginning: "Lady Marmalade" marked her segue into the realm of the sexy, lascivious vamp that would explode forth in *Stripped*. It marked the introduction of X-tina.

PIRATES SEEKING GOLD

Along with Aguilera's exploding fame and popularity came the vultures who sought to profit from the petite, blonde-haired, blue-eyed, big-voiced phenomenon. One day out of the blue, one of Aguilera's early demo recordings, "Just Be Free," suddenly appeared in some German record stores, produced and distributed by a company called Warlock Records. The tracks were recorded when Aguilera was 15 and were supposedly safely hidden away in the archives. RCA told the German record stores to pull what they had off the shelves. The plot thickened when RCA filed a breach of contract lawsuit against Warlock; however, in the midst of their dealings, the two companies came to a settlement so the recordings could be released as compiled into the album *Just Be Free*, which was released in 2001. To this day, the terms of the agreement remain confidential.[5]

Christina Aguilera, center, Mýa, left, and Lil' Kim accept their award for best pop collaboration with vocals for "Lady Marmalade" at the 44th Annual Grammy Awards in Los Angeles, February 27, 2002. AP Photo/Kevork Djansezian.

Separate from RCA, Aguilera filed several of her own lawsuits against Warlock, including breach of contract and unfair competition. These cases never came to trial, however, because again the parties settled, allowing the album to be released, additionally with permission from Aguilera for her photo on the album cover in return for a hefty sum in damages.[6] Of course, what is interesting is the question of what went on behind the scenes, specifically, why RCA and Aguilera so readily came to an agreement with Warlock. It's possible that the benefits garnered by her exposure in the European music scene with this album outweighed the alternatives of any potential lost income in the near term. However, with or without *Just Be Free*, the long-term potential for Aguilera's success was formidable.

STRIPPED **ERA, 2002–2003**

Just as she wished and like sands shifting in the desert, so did Aguilera's image change from the sweet little, pigtailed Mickey Mouse girl to the viperous vamp of her *Stripped* album. The album instigated a true potpourri of reaction including admiration, outrage, surprise, and disgust. But one thing was certain, Aguilera was not afraid of what anyone thought and was determined to be true to her art and her passions.

With step one, "Lady Marmalade," in the progression behind her and good girl and compliant singer gone, Aguilera lunged into the dark, yet creative world of *Stripped* and X-tina.

> At the time, I was under the thumb of my label, and I felt like I had to do, say, and act out everything they asked me to do. If they said, "Don't show your belly," I would [comply] [*sic*]. I was trying to please them and the public and finally I had to say, "Enough. I'm going to make a record that makes me happy and addresses all facets of being a woman. I don't care if I sell one or one million records." That's how I came to make *Stripped*.[7]

True to her desire, in *Stripped*, Aguilera shed her pure and pristine image to yield to her highly sexual and vampy self. In fact, in the "Dirrty" video, in addition to her costume—scant, open-crotched chaps and bra—she romped with another woman in a shower scene that is sensual, suggestive, and to some, shocking. Shock? Disgust? Call it what you will, but the government of Thailand became so outraged by Aguilera's presentation in this video that it banned all video from the public television networks. But was this the real reason "Dirrty," and all videos, were banned? In one scene in the "Dirrty" video, in the background there are two posters of Thailand promoting sex tourism and young girls.[8] Thailand has a long and seamy history of prostitution in general, but in particular, of child prostitution. Children under the age of 16 are bought and sold as slaves with estimates as high as 800,000 children currently in enslavement in the country. Child prostitution has become endemic to the economy of Thailand, surpassing the drug trade, sale of weapons, and even the lottery as a source of profitability.[9]

Aguilera is still banned from setting foot in the country. Given the circumstances, she is probably not too upset about that.

Stripped combined many musical styles and was an eclectic mix of rhythm and blues, gospel, soul, ballad, and hip-hop. Producer/songwriters Scott Storch and Linda Perry were the forces behind the scene of the album's success—including sales of 333,000 copies in its first week and achieving No. 2 on Billboard's Hot 100. Many fans, however, couldn't get past the images to get to the vocals. Aguilera was adamant about the important role of *Stripped* in her life, insisting that its sales success wasn't important to her: "*Stripped* had to be a truly experimental record and a true representation of me. I didn't care if I sold one or 1 million copies. It just had to be real."[10]

But in contrast to the heavy shock and criticism for "Dirrty," another song on the album, "Beautiful," received critical acclaim and earned Aguilera the Best Female Pop Vocal Performance Grammy in 2004. As well, in spite of the controversy surrounding the album and "Dirrty" videos, Aguilera went on to become the No. 1 Billboard Female Artist in 2003 for both the album and its singles with a total of 12 million copies sold worldwide.

Aguilera was quite vocal about her dissatisfaction with her first album (*Christina Aguilera*) and said: "I was playing a part dictated by my then manager and my record company. I hated who I was back then."[11] In fact, the title of the album *Stripped* came from the fact that she wanted to symbolically and publicly "shed her old skin."[12]

As the album attests to, if there's one thing Aguilera is not, it's inhibited. *Stripped,* and especially "Dirrty," are proof of her exhibitionist tendencies. She is so comfortable with herself, her body, and her body's biological functions that she has even been known to empty her bladder backstage, in a bucket, before a performance. "I'm very comfortable with my naked body. There's probably even some video of me peeing!" she said.[13]

Stripped recordings were as follows:

"Stripped, Pt. 1"	1:39
"Can't Hold Us Down"	4:15
"Walk Away"	5:47
"Fighter"	4:05

"Primer Amor Interlude"	0:53
"Infatuation"	4:17
"Loves Embrace Interlude"	0:46
"Loving Me for Me"	4:36
"Impossible"	4:14
"Underappreciated"	4:00
"Beautiful"	3:58
"Make Over"	4:12
"Cruz"	3:49
"Soar"	4:45
"Get Mine, Get Yours"	3:44
"Dirrty"	4:58
"Stripped, Pt. 2"	0:46
"The Voice Within"	5:04
"I'm OK"	5:19
"Keep on Singing My Song"	6:29

Aguilera amassed an impressive team indeed. She co-wrote most of the songs on the album, working with Perry, with whom she went on to work on later projects, Storch (of Justin Timberlake's "Cry Me a River" fame), and Matt Morris (appeared on *The New Mickey Mouse Club* at the same time as Aguilera, Spears, and Timberlake).

In looking at the titles of the songs, Aguilera's self-espoused story is quite clear, and its theme more than obvious. Clearly, here is a woman who professes her strength, her ability to move on, and her need to be loved for the person she is. And so she named the album *Stripped* because it was the symbol of what was happening in her life: "being emotionally stripped down and pretty bare to open my soul and heart."[14] A more specific revelation in this album of truth-telling is the song "I'm OK," which is about the time Aguilera's father hit her when she disturbed his nap. This incident was the catalyst for her mother finally deciding to leave the man who terrorized his family. This song was Aguilera's way of purging the incident and emerging a stronger and more powerful woman.

Besides a work of fine art, *Stripped* was also a work of fine therapy. While working with Perry on this album, Aguilera learned healthier ways of dealing with her emotions. Aguilera claims that Perry taught her that screaming was an effective release for stress and that she should "accept and embrace"[15] her mistakes to be an authentic person, comfortable within her own skin. Perry and Aguilera had a few things in common besides music, not the least of which was a Hispanic heritage. Perry's mother was born in Brazil and her father was of Portuguese descent. Also in common was their love of music at a young age. Perry followed in the footsteps of her father who worked as both an engineer and a performing musician and began focusing on developing her own talents after a difficult childhood struggling with kidney disease and addiction. At age 21 she moved to the Bay Area in California where she performed on street corners and ironically, like Aguilera, became known as "that chick with the big voice."[16] In addition and more recently, Perry focused on her songwriting talents, producing songs for Pink, Gwen Stefani, Courtney Love, Kelly Osbourne, Lisa Marie Presley, among others.

Despite its controversial reception, some of *Stripped*'s successes included that "Dirrty" became No. 1 in the United Kingdom, reached the Top 10 in the Netherlands, Spain, and Australia, but only made it to No. 48 on the Billboard Hot 100. *Rolling Stone* dubbed the "Dirrty" video the most played of all time. "Beautiful" reached No. 1 in the United Kingdom, Ireland, Australia, and Canada, and U.S. Top 40 as well as No. 2 on the Billboard Hot 100. "Fighter" hit No. 20 in the United States and the top 5 on world airplay charts. "Can't Hold Us Down," with Lil' Kim, was in the top 5 on world charts and the top 12 on the Billboard Top 100. "The Voice Within" was the second most played song on European radio in 2004 and No. 33 on the Billboard Hot 100.

However, of one thing there was no doubt, *Stripped* was a work of pure art and the representation of Aguilera's views on the role of women in today's society.

> Part of what I love about being an artist is being able to spark people's opinions, you know, give them something to talk about . . . to be able to spark conversation as to why, you know, why it is okay for a guy to be sexually open, but not a female? Why is it okay for a man to feel empowered from it, but not a woman?[17]

Stripped represented a huge turning point for Aguilera and probably the pivotal point in her anchoring as a solid, sensible, and grounded human being, traits very difficult, if not impossible, to achieve in the entertainment world. In fact, writer Elizabeth Day raised the question of whether Aguilera might have followed Britney Spears's nosedive had she not followed her muse and taken control of her career.[18]

Says MTV.com:

> While she may not be breaking the musical mode, she is dead set on breaking away from teen pop, and she stretches the genre's boundaries throughout *Stripped*, a highly personal proclamation of independence and adulthood.[19]

REVIEWS

Despite the art, despite the kudos, despite the rankings, *Stripped* fell victim to mixed reviews by the critics.

> In a review for *Rolling Stone*, Mike Rubin wrote that "Dirrty" was an unfortunate choice for the opening song, and that it essentially "misrepresents" the album. He said, "The title of *Stripped* screams, 'Look at my privates!' but the quieter message is, 'Be true to yourself.'" He credited most of the other songs on the album as being an artful combination of writing and singing, overshadowed by the sensationalism of "Dirrty."[20]

> In an interview with *Glamour* magazine, the question arose as to the controversy with *Stripped* and "Dirrty." Writer Laurie Sandell asked Aguilera:

> [Y]oung boys are watching the video, and they're not really seeing a strong, empowered woman—they're seeing a hot, practically naked woman dancing provocatively in a teeny bikini. How do you feel about that aspect of things?

Aguilera replied:

> Well, I can't control what they think. I'm not putting on a show for a guy; I'm comfortable with my body and it was a creative choice. I know that might make some women feel uncomfortable, but we need to stick together instead of getting angry at each

other for our choices. I think women are sensual, beautiful beings, and I feel empowered when I express myself sexually.[21]

Though at the time Aguilera insisted on strict artistic integrity as the driving force behind *Stripped*, in a "retrospect is golden" comment, she admitted that something more was going on with her at the time.

When I was 21 and made *Stripped*, I was pretty distraught about some personal issues coming up from my past. I was going out and partying a lot—as a lot of people do at that age—and did some very unhealthy things to deal with the pain. But I was able to say, "OK, hold on."[22]

THE BOYFRIEND

During the sexy, sultry time associated with her album *Stripped*, Aguilera took up with one of her backup dancers, Jorge Santos, about whom she wrote the songs "Infatuation" and "Underappreciated." "Infatuation" is about falling in love and "Underappreciated" is about falling out of love. The two dated for two years with the relationship ending in 2001, but Jorge continued on for another year as one of her backup dancers. Since this was her raunchy party stage, one can only surmise as to the nature and potential volatility of the relationship.

In addition to her confirmed relationship with Jorge, she was also rumored to have been linked with Carson Daly, Eminem, and Fred Durst of Limp Bizkit fame. About these alleged liaisons, which she admitted to sometimes urging on, Aguilera said:

I like to stir things up every once in a while and get a reaction. If I can't really date, at least I can think about it, or think about having crushes. It's just fun, and they never last very long, my crushes. It would be very nice if I could find the time to actually meet some really cool people, get to know them.[23]

"DIRRTY"

"Dirrty" cost a reputed and amazing $5 million to produce.[24] Although the entire album shook up the pop music scene, "Dirrty" was the shocker of any song, Aguilera's or otherwise, to that day. Commentary and reviews abounded, but MTV presented a written play-by-play, scene-by-scene preceded by this comment: "Christina Aguilera is a very bad girl . . . just ask her."

And so the proverbial envelope was pushed in a big way with the "Dirrty" video. Enter Aguilera in what became her (in)famous crotchless chaps, suddenly held captive in a cage. In an abrupt change of mood and costume, she appears dressed as a schoolgirl who boxes with a hooded, masked woman. Throughout, there are numerous actual and suggestive moves implying sexual behaviors, a female bodybuilder, a fire-eating woman, a man holding a chicken, people dressed in animal costumes, and finally, a wild scene in a men's room filled with romping and wild dancing, while Aguilera et al. "frolic near urinals while being sprayed with water . . . a reference to 'water sports,' a term for those who find pleasure in getting wet in, shall we say, 'unconventional' ways."[25]

Indeed, according to Corey Moss of MTV.com, this first song out of the *Stripped* album caused more controversy and instigated more talk, not all positive, than anyone thought. However, Moss points out that release number two from the album was "Beautiful," a far cry from "Dirrty" and a potential move toward damage control.[26]

However, according to RCA's then head of marketing, Dave Gottlieb, damage control was not exactly necessary, even though he admits that the single "Dirrty" did not do as well as hoped. Explaining the juxtaposition of the two releases, Gottleib said:

> It gives Aguilera the chance to explain herself beyond a party song and video that caused a lot of discussion. It lets her discuss the album more and it lets people in to how great an album it is and that it's not made up of 15 other songs just like "Dirrty," it's made up of 15 songs of all different types.[27]

BUT ON THE OTHER HAND . . .

However, there is always the other side, and is it possible that Aguilera *could have* defeated her self-proclaimed purpose of promoting the beauty of female sexuality? Was her promiscuous dress and behavior simply promoting the sexual abuse she so abhorred? Was she the epitome of

Russian writer Vladimir Nabokov's *Lolita* (1955), the sexually preco-cious young girl who attracts sexual perverts by her behavior? Was she exploiting herself, and by her very fame, encouraging young girls to adopt clothing and behavior that could indeed prove dangerous?

> The message from advertisers and mass media to girls (as eventual women) is they should always be sexually available, always have sex on their minds, be willing to be dominated and even sexually aggressed against, and they will be gazed upon as sexual objects.[28]

Aguilera has claimed she was simply exhibiting power as both a woman and an artist:

> [B]esides, what's wrong with a 22-year-old woman expressing her sexuality. It's not like I'm not of age and I don't know what I'm doing. The video [Dirrty] shows me in the power position. I'm not being objectified like all the girls in the videos of artists like Ricky Martin or pretty much any hip hop male artist you could name.[29]

Her explanation is plausible, but it leaves the question of all the viewers—in particular, the young viewers—who are not aware of Agui-lera's intentions with her sexuality.

JUSTIFIED AND *STRIPPED* TOUR

When Justin Timberlake made the announcement at the American Music Awards in 2003 that there would be a mystery pop-star sharing his summer tour, despite relentless prodding from reporters, he refused to name the star. However, star-studded event that it was, Aguilera, who was standing right behind Timberlake, unabashedly piped up that she was the one sharing his billing. From that point on, the paparazzi rumor mill raged that there was more than a professional pairing between the two and thus they became the item du jour. In the background of all this was Britney Spears who had just weathered a difficult and public break-up with Timberlake. Surely the announcement and pending tour was one more nail in the coffin of the destruction of the once-close re-lationship between the two women. However, according to Timberlake, the liaison between him and Aguilera had nothing to do with punishing his ex, which was the conclusion reached by Spears and others.[30]

And so, *Stripped*, "Dirrty," and "X-tina's" (her nickname due to her perceived X-rated performance of the songs in this sizzling new album) scantily clad self hit the road with Timberlake in a combined tour entitled "*Justified* and *Stripped* Tour." Timberlake was excited about the tour because he respected and enjoyed working with Aguilera, the one voice he felt was outstanding during their Mouseketeer days together. The tour went as scheduled except for a minor mishap on the stage in Atlantic City where some equipment was damaged and several shows canceled as a result.

Because of the tour's success, Aguilera and Timberlake were planning another tour in 2004, but when Aguilera announced that she had vocal cord injuries, it was canceled. However, it was suspected that the real reason for the cancellation might have been low ticket sales. Aguilera very publicly denied that this was the case yet subsequently went out on her own with the "*Stripped* World Tour" and a head full of black hair. The fans went wild, selling out most shows, and causing *Rolling Stone* to dub it the best tour of the year.

BAD GIRL

"We've always liked Christina Aguilera, so we were shocked to hear she's 'self-obsessed' and the 'diva from hell.'" That's what celebrated British photographer Rankin dubbed the "Dirrty" star, after working with her back in 2007. Rankin, who's snapped the likes of Spears, Kate Moss, and Leonardo DiCaprio, told *Closer* magazine:

> Aguilera was a diva from hell and pure torture to be around. She's so self-obsessed. She insisted that her chauffeur drive her indoors into the studio so she wasn't papped (snapped by the paparazzi)—even though there was nobody outside. Then, she crashed my after party and her bodyguard stood outside the bathroom shouting, "Nobody but Aguilera uses this toilet." She's a joke.[31]

Rankin is not the only journalist who has found Aguilera to be difficult. In fact, there are those who have dubbed her conceited and

Christina Aguilera performs the song "Dirrty" at Staples Center in Los Angeles as she opens the "Justified/Stripped" summer concert tour with Justin Timberlake, not shown, on June 16, 2003. AP Photo/Kevork Djansezian.

uncooperative. And woe to the writer who called her fat in the months after her baby was born![32]

Another nonfan is Fred Durst, one of the men Eminem had linked her with sexually in his song, "The Real Slim Shady." At the MTV Video Music Awards in 2000, Durst joined Aguilera in a duet performance, which Durst later bragged he did just to get some "nookie." Aguilera became furious and retorted, "He made such an ass out of himself and looks like a scumbag to everyone."[33]

On the other hand, and not too surprising, Durst had a retort of his own. He claimed that he said he would do a duet with Aguilera because the producers could not find her a solo slot, which upset her greatly. In fact, she did not attend the rehearsal because of his insults. He called her "ungrateful" and "spoiled rotten," and said, "She has a great talent, but she doesn't see what's in front of her because she's so young and dumb."[34]

Still in her Stripped and overtly sexual mode, it was rumored that Aguilera had bisexual tendencies. In fact, revisiting the "Dirrty" video, the choreography had her seducing both men and women. In early

2004 a British men's tabloid published an article about Aguilera claiming that she could be bisexual. It quoted her as saying: "I find it hornier looking at women than men. Sorry, I love experimenting with my sexuality. If that means girls, then so be it."[35]

Whether a mark of sexuality or not, there is one thing Aguilera is not short of and that is piercings. She has claimed that when she is having a bad day, she likes to go out and get pierced somewhere. Her more visible piercings are in her ears, nose, lower lip, and right nipple. There are others, and one in particular, diamond-studded, she claimed, is seen only by the doctor and some "selected" boyfriends. Aguilera said, "It's really beautiful and expensive, and I like it a lot."[36]

It would not be long before Aguilera ended up removing most of her piercings.

NOTES

1. Elizabeth Day, "I'm Not There to Parent Anybody's Children," *Observer Magazine*, November 23, 2008, LexisNexis para 7.

2. Ibid.

3. Ibid., LexisNexis para 8.

4. "Christina Aguilera," Gale Cengage Learning, n.d., retrieved March 24, 2010, from http://www.gale.cengage.com/free_resources/chh/bio/aguilera_c.htm.

5. "Christina Aguilera," CelebSpin.com, July 8, 2008, http://www.celebspin.com/2006/07/christina-aguilera/, retrieved August 26, 2009.

6. "Christina Aguilera," CelebSpin.com.

7. Laurie Sandell, "Christina: Intimate Talk about a Past That Still Hurts," Glamour.com, December 1, 2006, retrieved September 22, 2009, from http://www.glamour.com/magazine/2006/12/christina-aguilera.

8. "Thailand Upset by New Christina Aguilera Video," retrieved March 9, 2010, from http://www.buzzle.com/editorials/10-23-2002-28778.asp.

9. Sirirat Pusurinkham, "Child Prostitution in Thailand," retrieved March 25, 2010, from http://www.thewitness.org/agw/pusurinkham.121901.html.

10. Nick Duerden, "The Good, the Bad, and the Dirrty," Blender.com, November 15, 2003, retrieved March 9, 2010, from http://www.blender.com/guide/67285/good-bad-dirrty.html.

11. "Christina Aguilera Biography," 8notes.com, retrieved July 6, 2010, from http://www.8notes.com/biographies/aguilera.asp.

12. Adrian Thrills, "Britney? I Wish Her All the Best . . . Honest!," *Daily Mail* (London), November 7, 2008, LexisNexis para 34.

13. "Cristina Aguilera: Adult Swim," The Guide, http://www.blender.com/guide/68418/Aguilera-aguilera-adult-swim.html.

14. Jennifer Vineyard, "Aguilera Stands up for the Ladies, Discusses Father's Abuse," MTV.com, retrieved October 24, 2009, from http://www.mtv.com/news/articles/1458433/20021030/christina_Aguilera.jhtml.

15. Ibid.

16. "Linda Perry," retrieved March 7, 2010, from http://en.wikipedia.org/wiki/Linda_Perry.

17. Day, "I'm Not There to Parent Anybody's Children," Lexis-Nexis para 24.

18. Day, "I'm Not There to Parent Anybody's Children."

19. Vineyard, "Aguilera Stands up for the Ladies."

20. http://www.rollingstone.com/music/reviews/album/7733/37963.

21. Sandell, "Christina: Intimate Talk about a Past That Still Hurts."

22. Laurie Sandell, "Christina (without all the drama)," Glamour.com, July 1, 2008, retrieved October 11, 2009, from http://www.glamour.com/magazine/2008/07/christina-aguilera.

23. Richard Harrington, "Christina Aguilera's Fast Track: Ex-Mouseketeer Has the Voice to Pull Away from Teen Pop Pack," *Washington Post*, February 13, 2000, LexisNexis para 37.

24. "Christina Aguilera," Imdb.com, retrireved July 6, 2010, from http://www.imdb.com/name/nm0004694/bio.

25. Tanya Edwards, "How Dirty Is 'Dirrty'? X-posing the Kinks in X-tina's Video," MTV.com, retrieved November 10, 2009, from http://www.mtv.com/news/articles/1458275/20021022/christina_Aguilera.jhtml.

26. Corey Moss, "Christina Aguilera Follows Controversial 'Dirrty' with Inspirational 'Beautiful,' " MTV.com, retrieved October 24, 2009, from http://www.mtv.com/news/articles/1458506/20021104/christina_Aguilera.jhtml.

27. Ibid.

28. Debra Merskin, "Reviving Lolita?," *American Behavioral Scientist* 48, no. 1 (September 2004).

29. Angela Pulvirenti, "It Hurts So Much—I'm Not That Kind of Girl," *Sunday Telegraph Magazine* (Sydney, Australia), June 8, 2003.

30. Corey Moss, "Justified and Stripped Preview: Timberlake Talks Tour," MTV.com, retrieved October 24, 2009, from http://www.mtv.com/news/articles/1472259/20030603/timberlake_justin.jhtml.

31. http://www.absolutepictures.com/news.php?id=8576;byWENN, August 12, 2009.

32. Pulvirenti, "It Hurts So Much."

33. "Christina Aguilera Furious with Fred Durst," contactmusic.com, retrieved January 4, 2010, from http://www.contactmusic.com/new/xmlfeed.nsf/story/christina-aguilera-furious-with-fred-durst.

34. "Fred Durst on Christina Aguilera," Teen Music, retrieved January 4, 2010, from http://www.teenmusic.com/2002/06/03/fred-durst-on-Aguilera-aguilera.

35. "Christina Aguilera Biography," Christina Aguilera's Site, retrieved August 25, 2009, from http://www.simplyaguilera.com/.

36. "Christina Aguilera on Piercing," Teen Music, retrieved September 16, 2009, from http://www.teenmusic.com/2002/10/30/Christina-aguilera-on-piercing.

Chapter 6

BACK TO BASICS

From squeaky clean to freak queen . . . the diminutive pop chameleon's massive voice has been her strongest selling point in a music industry chock-full of fakes, floosies and mimes.[1]

Thus wrote Simon Collins in *The West Australian*. Aguilera is, if nothing else, her own woman: a woman who gets more comfortable in her own skin with each passing day. As she changes and grows, so does her music. *Back to Basics* followed the controversial *Stripped*, and it was a more mellow, albeit still innovative and eclectic combination of music including the sounds of blues, soul, Billie Holiday, and the Andrews Sisters. There were also echoes of Etta James and Marvin Gaye. "'I grew up listening to Etta James and Marvin Gaye and the great blues and soul singers,' she said. 'This was the music that nurtured me.'"[2]

Indeed, the sound she created was unique, a collection of finely sculptured tunes that paralleled her maturity of body, voice, and soul. In fact, she chose a relatively obscure music producer—DJ Premier— who was off the beaten track of big-name producers, such as Rodney Jerkins and Billy Mann, who were employed by the major music talents at that time including Beyoncé, Janet Jackson, and Jessica Simpson.

But what Premier had that the more famous producers didn't, and the reason Aguilera wanted him, was his ability to listen to both her music and her mind.

> "Premier really understood the record I wanted to make," Aguilera says. "I made a conscious decision to try and do a record that didn't sound like everything else out there. After a while, the big current-day producers have a very recognizable sound, and it all starts to sound the same."[3]

Premier, born Christopher Edward Martin, has been named as one of the top five producers of hip-hop ever by *The Source* magazine. Aguilera's choice, then, was certainly a significant deviation from the status quo and further evidence of her focused effort to find her own sound.

Likewise, along with her new sound came a new look: enter the Aguilera age of big blonde, big lips, and tons of red lipstick. Aguilera still reveled in her sexuality, though it was toned down from her *Stripped* days, but like her *Stripped* days, she relished being herself in every way.

Said Ron Fair, her former supporter at RCA Records:

> A lot of the girls who are in the sexy, MTV, hip-hop-pop-R&B category are relying on the same toolbox and the same color scheme. Aguilera has her own toolbox and her own color palette. Regardless of what happens commercially, her desired outcome is to gratify her muse.[4]

THE ALBUM

During the planning for the album, Aguilera consulted with Herbie Hancock, a fellow visionary and jazz artist, and Andrea Bocelli, an Italian tenor nominated three times for a Grammy. Bocelli has recorded more than 20 pop and classical albums, including seven complete operas. On the other end of the scale is jazz great Hancock, whose career, according to one biographer, has found broad success:

> Herbie Hancock's creative path has moved fluidly between almost every development in acoustic and electronic jazz and R&B since

1960. He has attained an enviable balance of commercial and artistic success, arriving at a point in his career where he ventures into every new project motivated purely by the desire to expand the boundaries of his creativity.[5]

Her taste in selecting these men to guide her was brilliant. Bocelli, blind since the age of 12, has the unusual achievement of being an accomplished singer of both opera and pop. Born in Tuscany, Italy, he has five albums in a variety of genres and has performed and recorded duets with Celine Dion and Sarah Brightman. Before changing careers to music, he studied law at the University of Pisa. Hancock, like Aguilera, was a child prodigy, having performed Mozart with the Chicago Symphony Orchestra at the age of just 11. He switched his genre to jazz in high school, formed his own group, and performed in clubs throughout the Chicago area. He's been known for his style: a blend of gospel, bebop, and blues. Bebop is a unique form of music that has a fast tempo and a prescribed structure and melody. With his first album recorded in 1962, Hancock now has 14 albums to his name.[6] Consulting with these gentlemen was testimony to Aguilera's desire to design "an innovative approach to honoring past eras."[7] She certainly made the right choices.

"*Back to Basics* is still a transitional record for Aguilera. Just as every other record she releases will be. Why? She's a born reinventor. Aguilera is not an artist who will ever be satisfied or settled,"[8] wrote Amanda Murray. Not satisfied, not settled, but, wrote Bill Lamb, certainly ahead of her time and in her own world:

> While the comparison may seem unusual at first, Christina Aguilera's *Back to Basics* is the most ambitious conceptual piece attempted by a major pop artist since Green Day's *American Idiot*. Like Green Day, Aguilera succeeds by stretching herself beyond the constraints of her past work and by looking back and pulling together personal influences from her past while knocking the ball out of the park with sincerity, emotion, and, yes, killer hooks.[9]

Reviewer Stephen Thomas Erlewine pointed out that the title alone, *Back to Basics*, is perhaps an indication that Aguilera might be "apologizing," or admitting that she went a little over the edge with *Stripped*. However, the song "Still Dirrty" qualifies her apology and loudly proclaims that she has not forsaken that image of herself that was embodied in *Stripped*.

> Sure, *Back to Basics* is way too long at two discs and some of it doesn't work quite as well as the rest, but it has far more hits than misses and it holds together as an artistic statement (certainly more so than any other album made by one of her teen pop peers). It may be all about style, it may be a little crass and self-centered, but it's also catchy, exciting, and unique. It's an album to build a career upon, which would be a remarkable achievement by any measure, but coming after the near career suicide of *Stripped*, it's all the more impressive.[10]

Back to Basics is a melding of all things wise and wonderful, and clearly all things Christina. The songs on disc one are primarily a celebration of her life and relationships. She includes several songs about her man and her marriage, one to her mother, and one to confirm her devotion to independence in art and spirit—a theme begun in *Stripped*, in particular with "Dirrty," and carried on with this album's "Still Dirrty":

> Don't tell me what to do
> Cause I'll never be uptight like you.

It is, say some critics, a unique and passionate way of honoring the music of past eras, a collection that excited her collaborators.
Said Premier:

> [S]he sent me some CDs of what kind of stuff's been inspiring her to make the record, and it happened to be a lot of stuff I grew up on in the early '70s, 'cause I'm 40. Aretha Franklin, Etta James, Marvin Gaye, Esther Williams, all kinds of different things. Once I saw that's the vibe she wanted, I still had to make it sound like the way my beats thump and stuff but still give her the atmosphere she's trying to bring out on the singing side.[11]

The first disc was the music of Premier while disc two was mostly that of Linda Perry who she worked with on *Stripped*. The sounds of the two discs are significantly different, but the combination unequivocally works. Frequent Aguilera journalist Corey Moss from MTV.com wrote:

"She played me the stuff Linda Perry did, and everything was dope, totally opposite from what music is, but when you put it all in the right sequence, it works," Premier said. "Her album is really, really well-rounded. She totally put it together right. And she was directing the whole thing. She knew what she wanted."[12]

From Perry's perspective:

"She's [Christina] got a lot of wonderful things to say," Perry said. "It was really easy to be a part of the record because she was so clear with her vision of the record and the ideas that she came with. All I did was sit and listen to her ideas and came up with a way to record it."[13]

Of her work with Perry, Aguilera said:

We creatively went into our own zone and our own world together. There are no cover songs so we made more of a '20s, '30s vibe with an authentic and organic twist.[14]

Aguilera was not merely inspired by the beautiful, smoky, and sensuous era of the 1930s and 1940s, she was truly impassioned about it. The music—soul, jazz, and blues—was "her" sound. But more than just sound, she wanted to create the atmosphere, the look, the feel, not only in the fashions as inspired by Veronica Lake, Marilyn Monroe, and Greta Garbo, but also the whole scene—the smoky rooms, the dimly lit clubs, and of course, the big, red lips that were the female trademark of the times. Her goal, though, was to create an entire vintage experience that went beyond the music. She sought to recreate "the experience" of the sultry, sexy, smoky 1920s through 1940s as well, therefore transporting her fans into a multidimensional fantasy land. In fact, it was the Golden Age—that classical era in Hollywood cinematography that captured the moods and atmosphere of that time frame, and it is said to have begun with the movie *The Jazz Singer* in 1927.

Why was she so rabid about the sound of that era? Aguilera said:

> There was such soul, emotion, and raw heart in it, so much real heart and emotion that's lacking in music today. You used to have to sing and convey emotion, and now, well, technically you can do anything with technology. It sucks for music today, but that's why that old music feels so good to me.[15]

How did a young woman from the 1980s–1990s become impassioned by the sounds of the 1920s through 1940s? Aguilera became introduced to the sounds of the era through her grandmother who used to look for and purchase vintage music of stars including Billie Holiday, Otis Redding, Marvin Gaye, Etta James, and Ella Fitzgerald; Aguilera often accompanied her on these outings. The two would then listen to the music together while Aguilera danced and performed on her living room stage. In fact, it was her grandmother who first noted that her granddaughter could really sing! Aguilera loved all of these artists, but the one who she grew up most admiring, and the one with the greatest impact on her work, was Etta James.

A TRUE THRILL

The thrill of a lifetime for Aguilera occurred in 2006 when Aguilera and James posed together for a photo spread for *InStyle* magazine. Anticipation for the meeting left Aguilera in a state of anxiety that only meeting one's idol can precipitate. But little did she know that the admiration was mutual. About Aguilera James said:

> When I first heard her stuff and saw her say on TV, [in response to the question] where she got her style, "I grew up on Etta James," that made me feel so good. . . . I couldn't believe that big sound, that big voice was coming out of her. Tell me who you've seen that sings like her, because we don't have anybody.[16]

Aguilera was overcome with emotion by James's comment and said, "I'm going to cry now."[17]

Just like between her and Perry, there are also parallels between James and Aguilera. Both women began singing as very young children, and for James it was as the five-year-old star of a church gospel choir. Soon she graduated to radio and at 12, she moved to San Francisco, formed a singing trio, and began working for famous blues bandleader, Johnny Otis. Throughout her career, she was known for "suggestive stage antics and a sassy attitude,"[18] a description that could surely apply to Aguilera as well. Peppered amidst her phenomenal successes was an addiction to heroin. Nevertheless, James won four Grammy Awards and 17 Blues Music Awards. A multi-hall-of-famer, in 1993 she was inducted into the Rock & Roll Hall of Fame; in 2001, the Blues Hall of Fame; and finally, in both 1999 and 2008, the Grammy Hall of Fame.

THE SONGS

As is most of her work, the songs on *Back to Basics* are autobiographical. In fact, these two songs were either about or influenced by her future husband, Jordan Bratman: "Save Me from Myself" and "Still Dirrty" (sequel to "Dirrty"). Next, "Oh Mother" was about the abuse in her childhood as well as her pride in her mother's strength in standing up to her father. For "I Got Trouble" she actually used vintage equipment so the song would sound like an authentic 1920s production.

"Ain't No Other Man," clearly a pivotal piece, represents, as Aguilera put it, her shift in real life from having men fall at her feet to instead pushing them away. It was also her way of celebrating her man, Bratman. As in everything she does, she also perfected the video version of this song, a sequence of dance moves taking the jazz era blues singer (Aguilera) from a world tour back home to the local joint where she catches up with local press and friends who enter in and out throughout the video. She finally runs into "the mystery man" in the bar and ends up pushing him away. All of Aguilera's moves are exquisitely choreographed and executed with the help of director Bryan Barber. She said, "It's all very planned out. I was very hands-on for this. I wanted to get every detail locked in just right."[19] In addition, the video depicts a mix

Christina Aguilera poses with the award for best female pop vocal performance for "Ain't No Other Man" at the 49th Annual Grammy Awards in Los Angeles, February 11, 2007. AP Photo/Kevork Djansezian.

of styles from the 1920s as well as modern, and also uses her alter ego, Baby Jane—on the stage door, license plate, and sheet music. However, who is Baby Jane and what she represents are secrets Aguilera has no plans to reveal. "I am Miss Baby Jane. . . . I'm not going to tell you why I have that nickname. I can't tell you. . . . It's still me, but it's me at this place in my life."[20]

Once more, Aguilera demonstrated her versatility and talent as a performer in her performance in the "Candyman" song and video. A symbol of her many personas, she appeared as a brunette, redhead, and blonde—all her real, natural hair and not some digital gimmick. She said that the three Christinas were a tribute to the Andrews Sisters and their 1941 song, "Boogie Woogie Bugle Boy."

About her three selves, Aguilera said:

The brunette, she wanted to be a little naughty, that was my X-tina days. She wanted to stir a little trouble. She was the third one to go up there so I think she was a little tired and tired of seeing everybody get the limelight. The redhead, she's looking over at the blonde and she's got a little jealousy in her, like, "Why aren't I singing the lead?" And the blonde is, of course, my side . . . kinda sweet and sassy at the same time.[21]

An interesting fact about recording this song was that not only did she need to learn to dance the jitterbug, she also needed to perform it three times, exactly the same, move-by-move, for each of her personas, in the dance routine. Then these three separate recordings needed to be perfectly melded together for the finished product. They were, and the final dance scene was flawless.

The song "Save Me from Myself" is all about her acknowledgment of Bratman's support of her complex and complicated life and self. She sings of gratitude for his support and patience, and even goes so far as to call him her savior, saving her from herself. The lyrics to this song are a mirror to their relationship. As evidenced in this song, her devotion is indisputable, but the question becomes, will the words and the truth they represent stand the test of time in a business where only the strongest relationships survive? Only time will tell.

A BROKEN LIAISON

Disagreements are common in the entertainment world, and one such disagreement put a wedge between Aguilera and her *Stripped* producer, Scott Storch. Storch, one of the top pop producers in the biz, produced seven songs on *Stripped* and publicly claimed to be one of the main reasons for the success of that album. Of course, Aguilera asked him to be involved with *Back to Basics*. But the plot thickened. Suddenly the deal was off, and as is standard in such dissolutions, the facts of the story differed significantly between Aguilera and Storch. According to Storch, the plans for *Basics* fell apart because Aguilera would not agree to pay airfare for him and his entourage to fly out to the recording sessions in California. On the other hand, according to Christina, Storch demanded to be ferried to California on a private jet, an expense she claimed was a lavish and unnecessary luxury. Whatever the case, the private jet was out, and so was Storch. As is true with most of *Basics*, the autobiographical theme prevailed as Aguilera celebrated the Storch incident with a track called "F.U.S.S.," which contains the lyrics, "Looks like I didn't need you / Still got the album out." Thus was the epithet to her former musical svengali.

But Storch, who worked with Aguilera's rival Paris Hilton on the single "Stars Are Blind," said:

> It's pretty pathetic that she would do a song like this. I worked on half of her last CD and sold her millions of copies. Obviously she cares more than I do that I didn't do this album, but I can't blame her, with an album full of fillers, over-singing, and lame Vegas-like cabaret music.[22]

With an impressive two discs, *Back to Basics* contains the following songs:

Disc One

"Intro (Back to Basics)"	1:47
"Makes Me Wanna Pray"	4:10
"Back in the Day"	4:13
"Ain't No Other Man"	3:49
"Understand"	3:46
"Slow Down Baby"	3:29
"Oh Mother"	3:46
"F.U.S.S."	2:21
"On Our Way"	3:36
"Without You"	3:56
"Still Dirrty"	3:46
"Here to Stay"	3:19
"Thank You (Dedication to Fans . . .)"	4:59

Disc Two

"Enter the Circus" (Performed by Linda Perry)	1:42
"Welcome"	2:42
"Candyman"	3:14
"Nasty, Naughty Boy"	4:45
"I Got Trouble"	3:42
"Hurt"	4:03
"Mercy on Me"	4:32
"Save Me from Myself"	3:13
"The Right Man"	3:51

CAN YOU JUDGE IT BY THE COVER?

Just as important to Aguilera as its musical contents, so too was the *Back to Basics* cover. Aguilera chose Ellen von Unwerth, her favorite photographer, to do the cover shot for *Basics*. Von Unwerth was known for being light and playful in her work, but she was a master at capturing a woman's sultry, sexy, erotic look, the main reason Aguilera wanted her. In fact, it was von Unwerth who photographed model Claudia Schiffer for the Guess? Jeans ads, after which she became known as one of the best photographers in the business. Von Unwerth's work was also regularly seen in *Vogue*, *Vanity Fair,* and other fine magazines.

So with Aguilera seeking to capture that Marilyn Monroe look, she and von Unwerth descended upon an historic Los Angeles hotel, the Hollywood Dell, as the perfect venue for supplying rooms that offered a unique, retro look and feel. On day one, Aguilera virtually spent the whole thing in bed, peering through the iron bars of a headboard and striking vampy, viperous, Marilyn Monroe poses. On day two, Aguilera and von Unwerth headed for a Los Angeles club, Forty Deuce, which features "a modern twist on a 1920s burlesque club,"[23] and provided the perfect ambiance for Aguilera's purposes. "'We got to play a little bit more of dress-up,' Aguilera said. 'A huge element also of this record is it's fun and playful, with a 1920's circus theme.'"[24] After several days of hard work, the winning cover photograph was one of Aguilera in bed, wearing a very modest white negligee, with a warm and inviting, but not really sexual, expression on her face. It was all about getting that Golden Age look and feel, and according to Aguilera, they succeeded in doing so.

SUCCESS

The stars were aglow as Aguilera set out about town, touting *Back to Basics*. In June 2006 she sang "Ain't No Other Man" at the MTV Movie Awards and the same month, she appeared on *Total Request Live* with some preview video clips from the album. In July there were concerts in Paris and London for which she sang both new songs from *Back to Basics* as well as several old singles. Then, in August, the album release party was held in New York City at which she performed a number of singles. Following were appearances on *Late Night with David Letter-*

Christina Aguilera appears on MTV's Total Request Live *at* MTV *studios in New York's Times Square, June 21, 2006. Aguilera's new music video* "Ain't No Other Man" *made its world debut on the show. AP Photo/Stephen Chernin.*

man, *Good Morning America*, the *Video Music Awards*, *Saturday Night Live*, and the *NBC Thanksgiving Special*, among others.

It's no surprise that *Back to Basics* was a tremendous hit that kept Aguilera riding on her magical and mighty wave of success. She was rabidly sought after by everyone, for everything. She in fact appeared on the covers of *Elle*, *GQ*, *GQ UK*, *Advocate*, *Allure*, *Attitude*, *Blender*, *Cosmogirl*, *Cosmopolitan*, *Glamour*, *Jane*, *AARP*, *Seventeen*, *Rolling Stone*, *InStyle*, and *Maxim*. For *Allure*, Aguilera's cover turned out to be the biggest-selling issue in its history.

The album itself was a worldwide hit, climbing to No. 1 in the United States, Great Britain, Australia, Germany, Canada, Switzerland, plus 11 more countries. It debuted at No. 1 on the U.S. Billboard 200 album chart, and was then the second No. 1 album of Aguilera's career. It also debuted at No. 2 on the Billboard R&B/Hip-Hop. It had the best sales week of her career with 346,000 copies sold in the United States and in 2006, it achieved the first-ever, biggest first-week sales by a female artist. Finally, as of November 2008, *Back to Basics* sold 3.7 million copies worldwide.

There was simply no end in sight for the Diva's upward climb.

NOTES

1. Simon Collins, "Cool, Slick Christina," *West Australian*, July 16, 2007, LexisNexis para 1.

2. "Christina Aguilera: Adult Swim," Blender.com, October 17, 2006, retrieved October 10, 2009, from http://www.blender.com/guide/68418/christina-aguilera-adult-swim.html.

3. Ibid.

4. Ibid.

5. "Biography," Herbie Hancock.com, retrieved March 11, 2010, from http://www.herbiehancock.com/bio/.

6. Herbie Hancock, Tripod.com, retrieved March 26, 2010, from http://airjudden.tripod.com/jazz/herbiehancock.html.

7. http://www.mtv.com/news/articles/1529698/20060427/aguilera_christina.jhtml. This page has moved and is no longer available.

8. Amanda Murray, "Back to Basics," August 27, 2006, retrieved October 12, 2009, from http://www.sputnikmusic.com/album.php?albumid=10534.

9. Bill Lamb, "Christina Aguilera: Back to Basics," retrieved October 13, 2009, from http://top40.about.com/od/albums/fr/caguilerabasics.htm.

10. Stephen Thomas Erlewine, "Christina Aguilera: Back to Basics," Mog.com, retrieved October 13, 2009, from http://mog.com/music/Christina_Aguilera/Back_to_Basics.

11. Corey Moss, "Christina's New Split Personality Is Mature and 'Dirrty,'" MTV.com, retrieved October 13, 2009, from http://www.mtv.com/news/articles/1529698/20060427/aguilera_christina.jhtml.

12. Ibid.

13. Ibid.

14. Corey Moss, "Aguilera Makes Her Comeback Twice as Nice by Expanding *Basics* into Double LP," MTV.com, retrieved October 12, 2009, from http://www.mtv.com/news/articles/1533622/20060605/aguilera_christina.jhtml.

15. Jennifer Vineyard, "Christina Aguilera Can Die Happy—She's Bonded with 'Bad Girl' Idol Etta James," MTV.com, retrieved October 25, 2009, from http://www.mtv.com/news/articles/1535359/20060628/aguilera_christina.jhtml.

16. Ibid.

17. Ibid.

18. "Etta James Biography," retrieved March 11, 2010, from http://www.biography.com/articles/Etta-James-9542558.

19. Jennifer Vineyard, "'Ain't No Other Man' Video Has Aguilera Singing the Blues," MTV.com, retrieved October 23, 2009, from http://www.mtv.com/news/articles/1534591/20060619/aguilera_christina.jhtml.

20. Ibid.

21. Corey Moss, "Xtina X Three: Aguilera Has Multiple Personality Disorder in Clip," MTV.com, retrieved October 24, 2009, from http://www.mtv.com/news/articles/1552870/20070220/aguilera_christina.jhtml.

22. "Aguilera and Ex-Producer in Feud," retrieved October 23, 2009, from http://ca.music.yahoo.com/read/news/35252516.

23. Corey Moss, "Aguilera Channels Marilyn Monroe for *Intimate* Album Cover," MTV.com, retrieved October 25, 2009, from http://www.mtv.com/news/articles/1535431/20060629/aguilera_christina.jhtml.

24. Ibid.

Chapter 7

FINDING TRUE LOVE

As is true with many celebrities, success in their careers usually does not equate to success and happiness in their personal lives, especially when it comes to finding true love. In fact, celebrities live exciting, fast-track, unreal lives that simply don't easily glide into the comparative serenity of the home and heart routine. To the point, writes Mark Frith: "Being famous may bring you vast wealth and lots of freebies but boy is it rubbish for your love life."[1]

Contributing to their higher-than-average divorce rates is that celebrities are used to moving through their lives in fast forward, and that also means with their relationships and marriages. They tend to jump into things, seeking the ultimate result in seconds without courtships over in what seems to be an instant. They assume that the thrills and excitement they encounter on the outside with the throngs of adoring fans will continue within the quiet confines of their homes. It doesn't.

Many celebs are driven, exhibitionistic risk-takers with tumultuous emotional lives . . . they can rarely relax and feel satisfied, and they don't feel secure with success, which in fact may not be lasting. They need a lot of affirmation, they worry a lot, talk about their anxieties. They need someone to listen and to reassure them.[2]

If Aguilera did indeed jump from one relationship to another seeking security and normalcy, it was not publicized in the way it is for other celebrities who have had myriad relationships and two, three, even four and five marriages. In fact, it seems to have been quite the opposite for Aguilera who found herself getting involved with people who wanted to exploit her, people who wanted to gain at her expense, and people who wanted to control her. Thus, she constructed walls that apparently grew higher with each hurt, whether business or personal. What was worse for her was her youth. As a young and attractive superstar, she was constantly being hit on by men twice her age, men who supposedly wanted to take care of her. "There's some really gross people out there," she said.[3]

So at a very young age Aguilera learned to close herself off from the sharks and predators; she learned not to trust and to isolate rather than be vulnerable in both her personal and professional lives.

> Before I met Bratman, I felt that I was the only person who was really going to be there for me, besides my immediate family. So I had to be strong, and I had all these walls up because I've been hurt so many times.[4]

JORDAN BRATMAN

Enter Jordan Bratman. Bratman was born on June 4, 1977, in the South Bronx, New York, to father Jack, a music producer, and homemaker mother, Gail. He and his brother, Josh, were raised Jewish. At 16, Bratman got his first exposure to the music business as an intern in a recording studio in New York City; surely his father had something to do with helping his son land this internship. The question is, though, was the music business something Bratman truly loved, or was he following his father's footsteps into a career with which he wasn't necessarily enamored?

In his younger years, Bratman attended the exclusive Ethical Culture Fieldston School, a private Jewish institution in New York City dedicated to guiding students to incorporating ethics into their lives. Dedicated to its students' Ivy League preparation, it was founded in 1878 and in 2004, had 1,600 students in pre-K through grade 12, although not all in one location. Some of the more notable graduates include Jill Abramson, managing editor for news for the *New York Times*; Nancy Cantor, chancellor, Syracuse University; Rob Glaser, Internet pioneer; Rodney Jones, jazz guitarist; Sean Ono Lennon, musician and son of John Lennon and Yoko Ono; and Belva Plain, author; among many others.[5]

The school's mission statement is as follows:

> The ideal of the school is to develop individuals who will be competent to change their environment to greater conformity with moral ideals.[6]

Bratman graduated from the school in 1995 and went to study business management at Tulane University's A. B. Freeman School in New Orleans. While a student at Tulane, he again became involved in the recording industry by discovering talented local musicians and singers and making recordings at the American Sector Recording Studio located in New Orleans.

In 1999, Bratman was appointed head of the artists and repertoire section of Darp Music Inc., a private music company located in Atlanta. His appointment was made by Grammy Award–winning producer, songwriter, and musician Dallas Austin. In fact, Austin produced works for Michael Jackson, TLC, Madonna, Pink, and many other notables. Under Bratman's leadership, the company thrived, a significant accomplishment in the tumultuous music business, and so Austin recruited Bratman to be his personal manager. In addition to managing Austin, Bratman also produced hits for the likes of Madonna, Michael Jackson, Pink, and of course, Aguilera.[7] Finally, Bratman moved to Los Angeles in 2002.

The Music Biz

The biz today is not what it was even 15 years ago when Bratman took his first steps into what was then a kinder, gentler industry. Since digital music had not come on the scene, the big record companies had only themselves to compete against, all with the same standard format—the vinyl record album in 33 rpm with the small single disks that played at 45 rpm, and of course, this evolved to the audio cassette. Like well-run companies anywhere, controlling costs was an important consideration, but with limited media and consumer purchasing options, record companies exercised the luxury of affording an artist several albums to "catch on" if they weren't an immediate hit. Back in the 1970s, Bruce Springsteen was one such artist.[8]

Fast forward to 2000 and the biz has been catapulted into chaos because of new, more economical options for consumers. As a result, the record company model has morphed from the big giants who controlled every aspect of production, marketing, distribution, and so on to iTunes and other Internet music providers that enable consumers to download their favorite tracks without purchasing an entire album. In fact, sales of new release albums have plummeted to 35 percent, which is the lowest since these Nielsen figures were tracked (1991). Likewise, sales of single songs exceeded $1 billion in 2009: the à la carte era of music had arrived.[9]

Enter the MySpace phenomenon. Although it has since become a mecca for social networking among friends and family, originally it was home to fledgling musicians who sought to present their work under their terms, with little or no cost, and without the loss of control signing with a record company meant. One wildly successful MySpace originating group was Hollywood Undead who acquired 20,000 "friends" in an amazing three weeks and in two months, their songs were played more than 1 million times.[10]

The bottom line is that the industry in which Bratman first interned and the one he works in today has drastically changed, the competition is savage, and in addition to à la carte, it is also the era of do-it-yourself.

In the old days, bands signed to a label, recorded an album, and toured in support of it. Nowadays, musicians have the option of signing to a label (large or small), relying on outside investment, or finding the time, energy, and money to manage everything themselves—the do-it-yourself approach.[11]

That Bratman has been a success in this chaotic and changing business is certainly an indication that he is a savvy and smart businessman, a fact that would certainly make him attractive to Aguilera. That Bratman is actively involved in handling aspects of Aguilera's business is heady stuff indeed.

THE PERFECT COUPLE

Love comes when you least expect it, and that was true for Aguilera. It was 2002 and Aguilera paid a normal visit to her management company, Azoff Music Management, owned by her then manager, Irving Azoff. While she was there, a dashing young man came by and Azoff introduced him to Aguilera. The dashing gent was Bratman.

At the time that they met, Aguilera was in her raunchy, sex-pot mode and in the midst of finishing up *Stripped.* In fact, Bratman and Aguilera got to know each other during some sessions for *Stripped*, which were recorded in the Darp studios. They became friends, but getting to the next level was a challenge for Bratman. Aguilera herself has said that at the time, she was "in a very closed place."[12] She was still reeling from the pain of the past in all its forms.

Finally Bratman succeeded in getting his friendship with Aguilera to the next level and the two started dating. Was it coincidence or did Aguilera's toned-down image, becoming sultry and sensuous as opposed to erotic and lewd, have anything to do with their relationship? For the next four years they dated steadily, and then, in February 2005, Aguilera entered a magic kingdom—and it wasn't Disney's. Bratman took her to Carmel-by-the-Sea, California, a quaint and beautiful California coastal town where Clint Eastwood was once mayor. Carmel is known as one of the most romantic getaways in the country, perhaps even the world, a reputation undoubtedly earned by its natural scenery and rich artistic history.[13] An interesting but little known fact about the town is that it has a law forbidding anyone from wearing high heels while walking on the sidewalks and streets without with a permit. Although the law is rarely enforced, the question certainly arises about Aguilera's preference for very high heels even with casual wear.

When they arrived at their hotel, Bratman opened the door to a room filled with rose petals and beautifully wrapped boxes. Aguilera was stunned. Bratman instructed her to unwrap each box, and inside each was a poem that he had written just for her. Finally there was just one box left. In a scene reminiscent from one of the world's most romantic movies, Aguilera said, "When I got to the last box, there was a ring in it. He got down on one knee and said, 'Will you do me the honor of being my wife?' I've been floating ever since."[14] Needless to say, her answer was a resounding "yes."

It is interesting to ponder that Aguilera's approach to her relationship with and subsequent marriage to Bratman was not at all like that of so many other celebrities where two-week courtships and multi-marriages are de rigueur. Long courtships, four years in their case, are the exception, and perhaps an optimistic omen for the longevity of their time together.

A PATH LINED WITH ROSE PETALS

Their wedding date neared and in April 2005, Bratman and Aguilera threw a party for the "meeting of the parents." Held in a Santa Monica restaurant, the couple went all out with more rose petals and mini-wedding cakes placed on all the tables. In his true romantic form, Bratman carried Aguilera over the threshold of the restaurant as they entered. Then, the next step in her journey to the altar was finding the perfect wedding dress. In July, Aguilera went to Paris for Fashion Week where she picked out her gown, which was designed by Christian Lacroix. The dress was quite elaborate, tight-fitting throughout the body with a very large and layered flounce at the bottom. Although certainly impressive, the look was something of the long pink gown worn by the classic Barbie doll.

As their November wedding date approached, and true to form and tradition, in September Aguilera traveled to Cabo San Lucas, Mexico, with several very special, select friends, to celebrate her upcoming marriage with her very own bachelorette party. With days spent relaxing by the pool and nights lapping up the foods, drinks, and breezes of the sultry evening salt air, the star spent time relaxing while spending quality time with her closest friends. She wore a tiara and veil the entire time, along with a necklace from which hung a huge "B" pendant. Then in October the couple threw a combined and wild bachelor/bachelorette party at the Hard Rock Hotel and Casino in Las Vegas.

With a Halloween costume party as the theme, the couple showed up as a medical team with Aguilera dressed up as a nurse, and Bratman, a doctor. As is typical of low-key, avoid-the-limelight Bratman, there was no record of a bachelor's party just for him, though it is likely that there was one.

And so the day was nigh. With the wedding to be held in the Napa Valley of California, the nation's primo wine country, a Friday night rehearsal dinner was held at the luxurious Auberge du Soleil Resort, a first-class hotel overlooking the beautiful valley and all its vineyards. Auberge du Soleil has an international reputation of excellence, and "as one of the world's best small luxury hotels."[15]

Wedding day: On Saturday, November 19, 2005, Aguilera, arriving with flourish and drama as only she could do, was ferried to her wedding in a white Rolls Royce Phantom. She emerged and began the march to join her husband to be. And then: beautiful bride, Christina Aguilera, and handsome groom, Jordan Bratman, were married at sunset in a tent by a mountainside forest, at the Staglin Family Vineyards in Rutherford. The wedding was a traditional Jewish ceremony, the first experience in Aguilera's adoption of Bratman's religious holidays, traditions, and ceremonies. Aguilera's bridesmaids were dressed in gowns designed by Stevie Wonder's wife, Kai Milla, and the couple's rings were designed by London-based jeweler Stephen Webster, as was Aguilera's five-carat diamond and platinum engagement ring.

The reception was what was described by guests as "lavish."[16] There were 130 guests and instead of presents, the married couple had requested that everyone contribute to the Hurricane Katrina and Rita relief funds. The published photos of the wedding show a marked contrast between the demeanors of the two. Bratman appears serious and almost reverent, while Aguilera appears almost flamboyant and as irreverent as Bratman is respectful.

Another question arises about religion. Although there is the early apparent element of the Mormon faith for Aguilera as a child, she was also reportedly raised Roman Catholic, one of the more dominant religions in mixed-faith marriages. Is there a contradiction in Aguilera's self-espoused newfound strength as embodied in her album *Back to Basics?* Are the normally treasured Christina holidays such as Christmas and Easter now a permanent part of her past? Or will the couple celebrate both sets of holidays as the years go on?

Singer Christina Aguilera and her husband, Jordan Bratman, attend the party after her New York concert at the Marquee Club, March 23, 2007. AP Photo/Dave Allocca, Marquee.

MARRIAGE

As their marriage began its roll down the runway, it became obvious to many Hollywood observers that it was off to a good start.

> In the two years since their wedding, Bratman and Aguilera have been regarded as one of Hollywood's most stable, low-profile couples. They have turned down numerous offers to document their marriage in a reality TV-show as Aguilera's friend, Jessica Simpson and her ex-husband, Nick Lachey, did in their show, "Newlyweds."[17]

But on the other hand, interfaith marriages are notorious for their high divorce rates. There is more than a difference in religion in these marriages, there is also the perhaps bigger issue of cultural differences. Says Georgetown University linguistics professor Deborah Tannen:

> People are so oriented to psychological interpretation that when a wife feels her husband isn't paying attention to her, she doesn't

realize it's because he has a different way of listening or of being involved in the conversation.[18]

One common area of conflict is in how children are raised. Not only is there the issue of which religion the children will be raised in, but there is the more subtle issue of discipline and expected differences in behavior. Another often unexpected source of conflict is in dealing with in-laws. Dealing with in-laws is one of society's more common sources of comic relief, but dealing with in-laws in interfaith marriages is far less likely to be a source of comic relief.[19]

Clearly, Bratman and Aguilera discussed and decided to celebrate Jewish customs, holidays, and to raise their children in the Jewish tradition, but one can't help but wonder what happened to the young woman who proclaimed her strength and independence in *Stripped* and who proudly announced the discovery of her cultural roots in *Mi Reflejo*. Did the damage of her childhood give her the predilection to defer to men? What did her mother think of her willingness to abandon the religion of her youth? Why was she so willing to discard her own traditions completely? Is this willingness to leave herself behind eventually going to backfire on her and her marriage?

In the meantime, what do Aguilera and Bratman do to nurture their fledgling marriage? Aguilera is very proud of one weekly ritual, one she has dubbed "naked Sundays."

> On Sundays we just do everything in the house, and we're just cozy and laid back, we don't need to go anywhere we're just with each other and have naked Sundays. We do everything naked. We cook naked.[20]

Aguilera calls Bratman her "rock," her stabilizing force, her human equalizer. Between Bratman, and baby Max Liron, her lifestyle has indeed changed drastically.

NOTES

1. Mark Frith, "Being a Star Is So Much Easier Than Working at a Marriage . . . ," *Belfast Telegraph*, October 17, 2008, retrieved October 23, 2008, from http://www.belfasttelegraph.co.uk/opinion/

being-a-star-is-so-much-easier-than-working-at-a-marriage-14007031. html?startindex=-1, para 19.

2. Joanne Kaufman, SPCL, "Middle Kingdom Family Matters: How Hollywood Marriages Fail," *Globe and Mail* (Canada), December 15, 1994, retrieved from LexisNexis para 9.

3. Jennifer Vineyard, "Christina Aguilera's Old Soul," MTV.com, retrieved October 24, 2009, from http://www.mtv.com/bands/a/Christina_Aguilera/news_feature_080906/. This site is no longer available.

4. Ibid.

5. "Ethical Culture Fieldston School," Wikipedia.com, retrieved March 21, 2010, from http://en.wikipedia.org/wiki/Ethical_Culture_Fieldston_School.

6. Ethical Culture Fieldston School Web site, retrieved January 6, 2010, from https://www.ecfs.org/about/missionhistory/mission.aspx.

7. "Jordan Bratman Bio," Yuddy.com, retrieved July 23, 2009, from http://www.yuddy.com/celebrity/jordan-bratman/bio.

8. Mina Kimes, "The Plan to Save the Music Biz," *Fortune*, January 18, 2010, retrieved September 1, 2009, from http://money.cnn.com/magazines/fortune/fortune_archive/2010/01/18/toc.html.

9. Ibid.

10. Ibid.

11. Aaron M. Cohen, "Reinventing the Music Business," *Futurist*, January/February 2010, retrieved July 13, 2009, from http://www.wfs.org/Dec09-Jan10/Music.htm, para 3.

12. "Christina Aguilera: Adult Swim," Blender.com, retrieved August 6, 2009, from http://www.blender.com/guide/68418/Christina-aguilera-adult-swim.html.

13. "Carmel-by-the-Sea, California," Wikipedia.com, retrieved January 22, 2010, from http://en.wikipedia.org/wiki/Carmel-by-the-Sea,_California.

14. "Christina Aguilera Marries," People.com, retrieved January 6, 2010, from http://www.people.com/people/article/0,,1131176,00.html?cid=redirect-articles/.

15. Calistoga Ranch, retrieved March 12, 2010, from http://www.calistogaranch.com/aubergeresorts.html.

16. Sheri Stritof and Bob Stritof, "Christina Aguilera and Jordan Bratman Marriage Profile," About.com Marriage, retrieved July 23, 2009, from http://marriage.about.com/od/entertainmen1/p/aguilera.htm.

17. "Jordan Bratman Bio," Yuddy.com.

18. Rebecca Kahlenberg, "The I Do's and Don'ts of Intercultural Marriage," Interfaith family.com, retrieved March 14, 2010, from http://www.interfaithfamily.com/relationships/marriage_and_relationships/The_I_Dos_and_Donts_of_Intercultural_Marriage.shtml.

19. "Jordan Bratman Bio," Yuddy.com.

20. Ibid.

Chapter 8

MOTHERHOOD

She rarely leaves the house. Her nails are blissfully unmanicured. She calls dates with her husband "Mommy and Daddy nights-out." Could the sexiest diva in the business have actually become a good girl?[1]

PREGNANCY

Max came along as a big surprise to Aguilera and Bratman, though a welcome one indeed. Aguilera was still on her *Back to Basics* tour when Bratman came to see her on her Washington, D.C., stop. The tour began on November 17, 2006, and had 17 stops in Europe, 16 stops in the United States, and 7 stops in Canada before the Washington stop. After Washington, there were 17 more stops in the United States, 8 in Asia, and 5 in Australia, with a wrap-up date of July 27, 2007. The singer had stopped taking the pill in order to rid her body of unnecessary hormones in preparation for becoming pregnant once the tour was over. Aguilera was certain she would not become pregnant right away. Wrong assumption. Although it is more likely that a woman will not become pregnant right after stopping the pill, approximately

50 percent will become pregnant within the first three cycles.[2] However, experts advise letting the body get back in its normal rhythm, which is evidently what Aguilera was trying to do, before trying to become pregnant.[3]

Nearing the end of the tour, one evening, just after arriving in Sydney from Brisbane, Aguilera's limo sped to the nearest Krispy Kreme donut shop. Bratman went into the store and emerged loaded up with a dozen mixed glazed donuts and two large coffees, presumably for him and Aguilera. At the time, she had not made any announcement about being pregnant, but the tummy bump and her highly unusual eating habits had the paparazzi in a frenzy of speculation.

Aguilera's stomach kept swelling and right along with it went the ongoing paparazzi frenzy. Then came one of the biggest faux pas that ever occurred in Hollywood: Paris Hilton's most unofficial and shocking announcement of Aguilera's pregnancy. It was true that Aguilera's stomach and eating habits had been rumor fodder for months, but by design, the couple had made no official announcement. That all changed the evening of the MTV Video Music Awards on September 9, 2007, when at a pre-award ceremony party, Hilton most shockingly delivered the news and basically hung Aguilera's private life out like laundry on the line. With microphone in hand, Hilton blurted:

Congratulations to the most beautiful pregnant woman in the world. You're gorgeous.[4]

With Bratman at her side, they first looked shocked, but quickly gathered their cool and handled the awkward moment by smiling with grace and aplomb.[5]

However, the question on everyone's minds: what was the big secret? The reason Aguilera had not wanted to announce her pregnancy was for safety reasons. When she learned she was pregnant, the tour still had a month to go, and the performances required 10 costume changes and several stunts that could be dangerous. She said: "There are so many things that could go wrong—somebody could slip, somebody could fall, I could fall. There was no way in hell I was going to jeopardize my baby for my show."[6] The show was, to say the least, arduous, and as always, Aguilera dazzled and stunned her audiences with her powerhouse lungs.

In addition were the spectacular effects of some acts including walking on stilts, tossing around blazing torches, and swinging from a trapeze. To ensure her safety and that of her baby, she wore a heart monitor during performances to constantly make certain everything was okay. She also canceled two shows in Australia after she fainted backstage due to an upper respiratory infection.[7] But despite these issues, she remained a true professional up to the very end; said one reviewer: "Aguilera's breathlessly energetic, senses-frazzling live spectacular of a concert brought the house down in Sydney, Australia."[8]

One very important part of pregnancy for most women is nesting, and Aguilera was no exception. A fan of the reality hit show, *The Osbournes*, Aguilera fell in love with the kitchen of the home, in which the show was shot. Aguilera, who tried never to miss an episode, said: "I used to look at the kitchen on that show, and they could hang out in that little sitting area. It looked really cozy."[9]

The Osbournes was a reality television program that was broadcast by MTV from March 2002 to March 2005. The show followed the lives of heavy metal singer Ozzy Osbourne, his wife and manager, Sharon, his son Jack, and his daughter Kelly. The couple has a second daughter, Aimee, who disagreed with the entire premise of the show and refused to participate. Much of the show revolved around conversations of daily life that took place in Aguilera's cozy nook. However, during its three-year run, the family very publicly grappled with serious life and death issues, including Sharon's cancer and Ozzy's ATV accident that nearly killed him. Taking advantage of her moment in the sun, Kelly embarked upon a short-lived singing career, the irony of which would soon be revealed. Ozzy was an icon in his own right, having been the singer with the heavy metal band Black Sabbath. Interestingly, long after the show was over, Ozzy admitted to the fact that he was stoned for just about every episode.[10]

When the Osbourne's house came up for sale, the young couple then bought it for $5.9 million.[11] Aguilera was ecstatic as she and Bratman planned all the rather major renovations they would undertake with their new home. Those renovations also became elaborate, a growing theme in Aguilera's life. The home's interior became dark with a heavy Victorian look in both furniture and accessories. It is also very opulent with an obvious display of the trappings of wealth.

BIRTH

The nest was ready, nook and all. Then, on January 12, 2008, at 10:05 P.M., Max Liron (in Latin and Hebrew, his name means "our greatest song") entered this world at Cedar-Sinai Medical Center in Los Angeles. Max was 6 pounds 2 ounces and 20.5 inches long. Interestingly, Aguilera was so terrified of giving birth vaginally that she opted for a Caesarean section. She said:

> I didn't want any surprises. Honestly, I didn't want any [vaginal] tearing. I had heard horror stories of women going in and having to have an emergency C-section [anyway]. The hardest part was deciding on his birthday. I wanted to leave it up to fate, but at the same time I was ready to be done early![12]

Aguilera was not alone in her preference for a C-section. In general, the rate of C-section births in the United States has risen to 29.1 percent of all births, a 40 percent increase between 1996 and 2004.[13] Although only a small subset of this total, there has been a rising trend among celebrities to opt for these planned births, some of whom include Britney Spears, Angelina Jolie, Madonna, Gwyneth Paltrow, and Victoria Beckham. Many people are critical of what they view as designer births, accusing mothers-to-be of trying to avoid stretch marks and having a C-section a month before what should have been full term. On the other hand, opting for a C-section is not all bad. Scott Serden, Clinical Chief of Obstetrics and Gynecology at Cedars-Sinai said: "If you want to look at what is the absolute safest [way to give birth], C-section without labor on an elective basis avoids all possible issues."[14]

Nevertheless, Aguilera remained afraid of giving birth. Despite her fears, Bratman was the stabilizing force for her during the birth and came complete with video camera to record the proceedings. When it was over, Aguilera said she found her peace in Max's first cry.

The new parents wanted to spread the news about their baby boy everywhere. The official spokesperson message was: "Christina Aguilera and Jordan Bratman are proud to announce the birth of their son Max Liron Bratman. He is a beautiful, healthy baby boy. Mother is resting and doing well."[15] Then, on her Web site, along with images of blue balloons, she posted: "Today is a very special and joyful day for Jordan and I as we welcome our first son into this world."[16] In addition, and in gratitude to her fans for their loyalty and support, she posted video footage of her song "Save Me from Myself," from *Back to Basics*. The video included footage from her and Bratman's wedding. She wrote: "Just a little something to say 'thank you' for your undying love and support. It is in no small part because of you that I live such a blessed and wonderful life."[17] Her gratefulness to her fans is notably in contrast to her much-criticized behavior during "meet 'n greets" earlier in her career.

In addition, because Aguilera's fans were so rabid about sharing this event with her and seeing her baby, *People* magazine offered the couple $1.5 million for Max's baby pictures, the fifth-highest sum paid for baby photos. But sales of the issue fell short of the magazine's hopes and expectations.[18]

Not surprising, since Cedar-Sinai is the hospital of choice for so many celebrities, Aguilera had company during her hospital stay: Nicole Richie, daughter of Lionel Richie, gave birth on the same day and the same floor as Aguilera. Richie and her husband, Joel Madden, lead singer of the band Good Charlotte, welcomed their baby daughter, Harlow Winter Kate Madden.[19] There was also a veritable baby boom going on that year as, among many others, Jennifer Lopez gave birth to twins, Halle Berry, a baby girl, Cate Blanchett had a boy, Tori Spelling, a girl, and Gwen Stefani, a little boy.[20]

POSTPREGNANCY: GETTING IN SHAPE

In an interview with *Glamour* magazine, Aguilera discussed some post-pregnancy issues relative to getting back in shape. However, writer Laurie Sandell first made an interesting observation about Aguilera's pre- and postbirth interpersonal behaviors:

> She rarely met my eyes during the interview—a technique she told me at the time that helped her gather her thoughts—and while she was articulate, she seemed to choose her words very carefully. Almost two years later, I meet a very different Aguilera: The first thing I notice is she looks me directly in the eyes—a nice improvement.[21]

Aguilera has often pronounced herself as shy, something many find hard to believe while watching her belt out song after song and prancing around in skimpy costumes, ever-present belly in display. However, shy isn't necessarily shy in all contexts:

> As with many psychological conditions, the symptoms of social phobia lie on a spectrum of severity. Some people experience the anxiety only in specific situations—talking on the phone, for example, or using a public restroom. Others have a more generalized phobia that makes most kinds of human interaction stressful. Still others may be comfortable onstage and yet have trouble with one-on-one encounters.[22]

So it can be said that part of Aguilera's postpregnancy shape-up was not merely physical. It is probable that with the birth of her son also came a newfound confidence that usurped the shyness that controlled her before.

Along with newfound confidence, Aguilera gained 40 pounds during her pregnancy and most of the extra after-birth pounds were in her belly. By way of comparison, the average amount of weight gained by women during pregnancy is 25 to 35 pounds.[23] There was also the ongoing issue that she loved to eat. Aguilera said: "Diet is not a word in my vocabulary—I don't like depriving myself of things."[24]

So began the exercise program, complete with personal trainer, who, of course, came to her house for the workout sessions. Each workout session was 90 minutes long, and she engaged in five sessions per week. But there was one major problem, and that was that Aguilera hated to exercise. On the other hand, she wanted results and she wanted them right away.

> Being the perfectionist that I am, my attitude was, this had better hurry up—I want results! My trainer kept saying, "Give it time, you're looking great." Everyone around me was saying they could see a difference, but, you know, you're hardest on yourself. I did see my stomach get flatter and tighter and more muscle definition.[25]

Also during her pregnancy, Aguilera's feet also swelled from size five to seven, a fact that concerned her greatly considering her expansive shoe collection. Fortunately, she returned to prepregnancy size shortly after giving birth. But one change Aguilera embraced wholeheartedly was the change in her breasts postpregnancy. In fact, she actually required a size E cup!

> It's kind of hilarious! I've never fit into an E-cup before. I look at my husband and go "Guess what size this bra is?" And when I tell him, he's just amazed. We have kept the tags to prove it, to look back for memory's sake.[26]

In addition to her exercise program, Aguilera credits breast-feeding for her weight loss. And although this has not been officially researched, she is not alone in making this conclusion. It has long been suspected that breast-feeding gives mothers an edge in shedding baby weight. But lately, a parade of celebrities has attributed their postpartum slimming to nursing, bringing this age-old topic back into the spotlight. Adding to the conversation is a large study that suggests that weight loss through breast-feeding is not a myth.

> Earlier this year, Rebecca Romijn, who wore a shrink-wrapped outfit in "X-Men," called breast-feeding her new twins "the very best diet I've been on." After Angelina Jolie posed for the November 2008 cover of *W* magazine nursing one of her twins, she said that it had helped her regain her figure. (That cover made her an icon among breast-feeding advocates and inspired a bronze statue of a nude Ms. Jolie double-nursing her newborns that was exhibited in London last month.)[27]

CHANGES

Although their lives are glamorized and envied by their fans, celebrities have to deal with a myriad of changes when they enter the sacred world of motherhood. An interview with several "big name moms" yielded the following "five paramount parenting challenges."[28]

1. When to have the baby: When you're a star, a lengthy absence rarely makes the public's heart grow fonder. And that's why celebrities carefully plan just when to take big chunks of time off to have a child.

2. Shaping up: When it comes to shedding post baby weight, there's no grace period for actresses, who stake much of their career on their appearance.

3. Getting back on the set: Stars get to schlep their kids to movie and sitcom sets with them, which makes going back to work that much easier.

4. Hiring the nanny: Yes, well-compensated stars can pay top dollar for the very best in baby care. But they still need to worry about finding loveable, reliable caregivers who won't sell them out to the tabloids and will take great care of the kids.[29]

After becoming a mother, Aguilera's lifestyle, and outlook on life in general, changed significantly. Perhaps one of the biggest changes was her newfound calmness, and because of her own chaotic upbringing, she became fanatical about producing a calm and peaceful environment for her son to grow up in.[30] But on the other hand, she has also said she played rock music to her baby, including the likes of Led Zeppelin, Rolling Stones, and Metallica.[31] Perhaps what she really sought was balance in her home atmosphere.

Another major change in Aguilera's life was her bedtime. As are many performance artists, Aguilera was nocturnal, with a usual bedtime of three or four in the morning. The night, she claimed, was the time when her creative juices ran most freely. Now, however, since she gets up with Max at six each morning, her bedtime has changed to midnight. But what has not changed is Aguilera's love of her bed. Her favorite times with baby Max are when the two are cozy in bed together. In fact, Aguilera has said, bed is her very favorite place to be and if she could, she would do everything from bed.[32] In fact, the bed in which they snuggle looks very similar to a medieval throne. It is a very extravagant four-poster monster replete with monarch-style canopy with sheer black shrouds that can either be tied back or let free to surround the entire bed. Aguilera has even said she wanted a bed where she could feel like "a queen on a throne."[33]

But she is also realistic about the new demands of being a mother on her life. "Being a singer and a mother is a juggling act, but doing both comes naturally. Now, I couldn't do one without the other."[34] And as with everything she does, Aguilera has strong views about motherhood, including the need to keep a strong sense of self and career. She said, "I'd never give up my musical or artistic side to be a mother. There's got to be a balance and I want to set that example—as the kind of woman I want my son to respect."[35]

It's called "the glamorization of motherhood and the fixation on celebrity mothers."[36] The world is indeed fixated on celebrity mothers who seem to do it all so effortlessly, and always with a smile on their face and bounce in their walk. Albeit, as young Max Liron grows out of babyhood and into toddlerhood, Aguilera appears to struggle under his increasing size and weight sporting still the smile, but minus the bounce.

However, it seems rather peculiar that there is never any nuance as to anything but joy and glamour when it comes to celebrity motherhood. What about the stretch marks, depression, morning sickness, and utter exhaustion that comes with motherhood for the masses? Karen Brooks writes about the celebrity magic wand that on the surface makes the stars impervious to the yucky part of pregnancy and motherhood:

> Parenthood is different for these fabulously wealthy and privileged beings. Not only can they afford to take time from their "horrendous" schedules to enjoy simply being "mum," their bodies snap back into shape (with the help of chefs and trainers) and their nights are uninterrupted as the hired help rises to attend to the newborn. Now that's fine when your face and body are your ticket to success, but to suggest that this is "normal" and that we too can experience the pleasures of this kind of parenthood is completely unrealistic.[37]

The message here is that, unfortunately, the everywhere vision of successful, smiling, and self-assured celebs toting their not-yet so successful, smiling, and self-assured cherubs creates a false perception of what motherhood is like for the masses. Writes Brooks: "Pretending that pregnancy and childbirth is like a Disney movie, with happy endings and where everything fundamentally stays the same, only better, sets up unrealistic expectations and eclipses the realities of bringing a child into this world."[38]

Other than Aguilera, what's the word from the celebrity front about motherhood and career?

Jennifer Lopez, who had twins in 2008 and whose "whole world has changed"[39] said:

I'm still figuring it out. It's hard to even be away from them when I'm getting my hair and makeup done. I keep putting them on my lap, and the makeup artist is like "Um, can you move her?" And I'm like "No! And you know what? I have to have two babies on my lap!" But it's part of being a mom. My whole world has changed. It's going to affect every single decision of my life.[40]

Nicole Kidman said about her baby with Keith Urban, Sunday Rose:

"I don't ever leave her. No, no. I like her here," said Kidman in an emerald Prada dress. "I fly back home (Nashville) tomorrow; I spend the bulk of my time in Tennessee, but I still have to have her with me. Being a mom is the norm. So many women . . . have their toe at least in the workforce and they still want to have families. That's me, too."[41]

Finally, Halle Berry said of finding the right work-life balance since her daughter Nahla was born:

I'm only seven months into learning how to balance those things. What I know for sure is that many women have done it before me, so it's doable. And I'm not too panicked about it. I'm learning as I'm going. I'm a newbie, and I'm making a lot of mistakes right now.[42]

As for Aguilera, her nights of star-studded, glamorous parties have been replaced by scrapbooking and other "Mommy" activities. Indeed, hermit was the watchword as she admitted that there was no real reason for her to ever leave her home. Aguilera is also adamant that her marriage has grown stronger since little Max was born. A child, she said, is a constant reminder of the love between two people as well as a never-ending work-in-progress. "It can be very challenging. It can be incredible and exciting."[43]

Perhaps a major reason for Aguilera's enriched marriage is her belief that truly nurturing her sexuality as a woman and mother is something not only important to her own personal growth and satisfaction, but also for the sake of her son: "But more than ever, women are coming out and owning their sexuality and feeling good about it. I want my son to grow up respecting that."[44]

Thus, a simple life prevails, at least for the present, and Aguilera prefers to stay close to home, enjoying lone strolls on the grounds of her and Bratman's property, handling a variety of projects she's become involved in, and working on recordings for her new album in the privacy of her backyard recording studio. In fact, the paparazzi that normally followed her pester Bratman when he leaves the house that they haven't seen Aguilera in days. Like all mothers who dream of working from home, her backyard studio is her dream-come-true, allowing her to seamlessly combine her personal and professional lives "and it has just been so perfect for me to just wake up in the morning, put on my flip flops and sweat pants, and just go back in the studio and pretty much get into my creative cave and zone out that way, so it's been really convenient."[45] Then in the evenings, after Max has been put to bed, she engages in her workout to get back in shape from the 40 pounds she gained during her pregnancy. Forty pounds on a 5-foot-2-inch frame is a lot.

"Since becoming a mum, I feel I have more knowledge and that makes me feel beautiful. I feel more centered which makes me feel confident and sexy."[46]

MAX LIRON

Eight days after his birth was the first ceremony Aguilera and Bratman celebrated in their baby's life: that of the bris: a Jewish ceremony that celebrates the circumcision and naming of a baby boy. The timing of the ceremony—eight days after a baby is born—symbolically commemorates the seven days of creation with the eighth day representing transcendence from the physical world to the metaphysical world. Therefore, it is at this time when the union of body and soul can take place.[47] Although Aguilera was brought up Roman Catholic, she adopted Bratman's Jewish faith involving holidays and customs. The bris was held on January 20, and for the event, Aguilera decorated their home with penis balloons. "We're such a non-conventional couple, we had a lot of penis balloons everywhere."[48]

When Max reached 16 months, he became fixated on cleaning the house, and in fact, according to Aguilera, one of his first words was "vacuum."[49] Aguilera also admitted that she and her husband have to watch what they say around Max because he picks up everything, including a little Spanish, spoken in celebration of his Latin heritage.

Since then, little Max is constantly photographed out and about in Los Angeles in his mother's arms, including dressed up for Halloween parties and shopping for Christmas trees. Thus, in addition to his Jewish upbringing, Max is, at the very least, going to be exposed to Christian traditions. Aguilera said that the most memorable moments of 2009 for her were celebrating Christmas with Max: "That was the best memory, his face and seeing his everything come to life with Santa. . . . It was really amazing."[50]

In fact, as he passed his second birthday, it looked as if Aguilera was beginning to struggle carrying him as he morphs from little baby to rugged toddler. But there is no doubt of one thing, Aguilera looks the part of a very devoted mother.

NOTES

1. Laurie Sandell, "Christina (without all the drama)," Glamour. com, July 1, 2008, retrieved August 25, 2009, from http://www.glamour. com/magazine/2008/07/christina-aguilera.

2. "How Long after Being on Birth Control Can I Get Pregnant?," Baby Hopes.com, retrieved March 15, 2010, from http://www.baby hopes.com/articles/birth-control.html.

3. "The Pill and Pregnancy," Pregnancy-info.net, retrieved March 15, 2010, from http://www.pregnancy-info.net/pregnancy_pill.html.

4. Brian Orloff and Mike Fleeman, "Paris Hilton Makes a Baby Announcement—for Christina Aguilera," People.com, retrieved March 15, 2010, from http://www.people.com/people/package/article/0,,20053775_20055465,00.html.

5. Shawn Adler, "Christina Aguilera's Pregnancy Was a Surprise, Singer Reveals to Marie Claire," MTV.com, retrieved October 24, 2009,

from http://www.mtv.com/news/articles/1575234/20071128/Christina_Aguilera.jhtml.

6. Ibid.

7. "Aguilera Definitely Wants Kids to Be Bilingual," *Hindustan Times*, August 10, 2007, LexisNexis.

8. cdUniverse, Music, retrieved March 15, 2010, from http://www.cduniverse.com/productinfo.asp?pid=7533040.

9. "Aguilera Fell in Love with Ozzy's Kitchen on TV," WENN Entertainment News Wire Service, December 24, 2007.

10. "The Osbournes," Answers.com, retrieved March 20, 2010, from http://www.answers.com/topic/the-osbournes.

11. "Ozzy Sells 'The Osbourne' Mansion to Aguilera," *Hindustan Times*, September 24, 2007, LexisNexis.

12. "X-Tina Dishes on Her Issues—Down There," VH1.com, retrieved March 15, 2010, from http://blog.vh1.com/2008-02-15/x-tina-dishes-on-her-issues-down-there/.

13. Louise Chang, reviewed by, "Elective Cesarean: Babies on Demand," WebMD.com, retrieved March 15, 2010, from http://www.webmd.com/baby/features/elective-cesarean-babies-on-demand.

14. Jennifer D'Angelo, "Birth by Design: Are Celebs Too Posh to Push?" Foxnews.com, retrieved March 20, 2010, from http://www.foxnews.com/story/0,2933,88505,00.html.

15. "Christina Aguilera Celebrates Birth by Releasing Private Video Footage," *New Zealand Herald*, January 15, 2008, LexisNexis para 4.

16. Ibid., para 5.

17. Ibid., para 7.

18. Lacey Rose, "The Most Expensive Celebrity Baby Photos," Forbes.com, retrieved January 12, 2010, from http://www.forbes.com/2008/04/10/hollywood-celebrity-magazines-biz-media-cx_lr_0410babypix.html.

19. CBC Arts, "Nicole Richie, Christina Aguilera Deliver Babies in Same Ward," *CBC News*, January 12, 2008.

20. "The 2008 Celebrity Baby Boom," retrieved March 15, 2010, from http://fametastic.co.uk/2008-celebrity-baby-boom/.

21. Sandell, "Christina (without all the drama)."

22. Matthew Schulman, "Being More Than Merely Shy," *U.S. News and World Report*, April 28, 2008, retrieved January 3, 2010, from http://health.usnews.com/health-news/family-health/articles/2008/04/17/more-than-shy-how-to-cope-with-social-anxiety.html, para 5.

23. "Pregnancy and Weight Gain," WebMD.com, retrieved March 15, 2010, from http://www.webmd.com/baby/guide/healthy-weight-gain.

24. Maureen Paton, "Genius in a Bottle: Christina Aguilera Celebrates Her Wild Side with Her New Fragrance," MailOnline, retrieved December 3, 2009, from http://www.dailymail.co.uk/home/you/article-1223831/Christina-Aguilera-celebrates-wild-new-fragrance.html.

25. Sandell, "Christina (without all the drama)."

26. "Aguilera Credits Breastfeeding for Figure Reversal," *New Zealand Herald*, May 23, 2008, retrieved November 14, 2008, from http://www.nzherald.co.nz/entertainment/news/article.cfm?c_id=1501119&objectid=10512068, para 7.

27. Catherine St. Louis, "Breast-Feed the Baby, Skip the Dieting?" *New York Times*, November 12, 2009, E3.

28. Donna Freydkin, "Celebrity Moms Go through Changes," *USA Today*, August 6, 2004, retrieved June 24, 2009, from http://www.usatoday.com/life/people/2004-08-05-celeb-moms_x.htm, para 3.

29. Ibid., paras 4–13.

30. "Christina Aguilera Says Becoming a Mom Has Stopped Her from Being Loud and Impatient," *Daily News* (New York), March 15, 2009.

31. Nadia Arsalance, "Rockin' Baby," *West Australian*, February 23, 2008.

32. Philipa Bourke, "Christina Aguilera's Boudoir Hang-Out," National Ledger.com, retrieved December 2, 2009, from http://www.nationalledger.com/artman/publish/article_272628805.shtml.

33. "Inside X-Tina's Beverly Hills Home," retrieved March 15, 2010, from http://omg.yahoo.com/blogs/pepsi/inside-xtinas-beverly-hills-home/39?nc.

34. Adrian Thrills, "Britney? I Wish Her All the Best . . . Honest!" *Daily Mail* (London), November 7, 2008, LexisNexis para 21.

35. "Christina Aguilera Urges Mothers to See the Importance of Balance," kiddicare.com, retrieved October 17, 2009, from http://www.kiddicare.com/webapp/wcs/stores/servlet/newsarticle0_96864_10751_-1_10001.

36. Naomi Wolf, "The Motherhood Myth," *Times* (London), March 24, 2001, LexisNexis para 6.

37. Karen Brooks, "Smooth out the Bumps," *Courier Mail* (Australia), January 16, 2008, LexisNexis para 12.

38. Ibid.

39. Kelly Carter, "The Mother of All Parties," *USA Today*, October 8, 2008.

40. Ibid.

41. Ibid.

42. Ibid.

43. Elizabeth Day, "I'm Not There to Parent Anybody's Children," *Observer Magazine*, November 23, 2008, LexisNexis para 34.

44. Paton, "Genius in a Bottle."

45. Fekadu, Mesfin, "Christina Aguilera Becomes DJ, Talks Music, Film," Las Cruces Sun-News.com, retrieved August 7, 2009, from http://www.lcsun-news.com/fdcp?1249652156842.

46. "Christina Aguilera Feels Sexier as a Mum," retrieved August 7, 2009, from http://www.thaindian.com/newsportal/entertainment/Christina-aguilera-feels-sexier-as-a-mum_100228782.html.

47. "The Bris," Rabbi Yehuda Lebovics, retrieved March 15, 2010, from http://www.torahview.com/bris/html/the_bris.html.

48. "Penis Balloons Welcome Aguilera's Baby to Judaism," WENN Entertainment News Wire Service, February 5, 2008, LexisNexis.

49. "Christina Aguilera's Cleaner Son," China Daily.com, retrieved November 22, 2009, from http://www.chinadaily.com.cn/showbiz/2009-05/13/content_7772436.htm.

50. Mark Gray, "Christina Aguilera's Resolution Is to Continue the Good Times," People.com, retrieved March 15, 2010, from http://www.people.com/people/article/0,,20334092,00.html.

Chapter 9

WHAT'S AHEAD?

Though Aguilera said that motherhood would slow her down, it nevertheless appears that her fast track remains in high gear and on course. First is her sixth album, *Bionic*, released in June 2010. Then there is her first acting role in the motion picture *Burlesque*, due for release in November 2010. Finally are her involvements in the Yums! World Hunger Relief Program, the launch of her own radio station, her three fragrances, and a youth voting campaign, Rock the Vote. There is more, but even this is certainly a list that is exhaustive simply to read.

WORKING WITH TARGET

It was on November 11, 2008, that *Keeps Gettin' Better: A Decade of Hits*, a collection of her songs put together in an album, was released and made available only through Target stores. Besides being an obviously good and lucrative business deal, the selection of Target was significant. Aguilera is involved in all her own decisions and coincidence or not, Target has achieved a reputation of offering quality merchandise at competitive prices, and in the clothing end, it's particularly known for its "cheap chic"[1] and "fast fashion."[2]

What is cheap chic? The cheap chic trend is all about offering designer clothes for much, much less and moving them in and out of stores in considerably less time than the standard store six-month seasonal shelf life. The argument is that although such retailers end up reducing prices by almost 50 percent, consumers become bored by the stale merchandise.[3] On the other hand, the innovators of fast fashion retailers, namely Target and H&M, have teamed up with designers: Proenza Schouler for Target and Roberto Cavalli and others for H&M to engage in a much different model where cheaply made but haute couture styles bring "the look of the moment to Main Street."[4] Unlike traditional, season-based shelf strategies, fast fashion operates on a move-em-in, move-em-out plan. Also, for the designers it is a matter of exposure and recognition in a market that has most likely never heard of them. However, in 2008 and amidst a significant recession, the argument has been raised about the ethics of manufacturing great quantities of these trendy styles in places like China and Romania where labor is cheap and workers exploited. Of course, this argument is raised by high-profile designers such as Donatella Versace.[5]

It is unquestionable that chic is certainly what Aguilera is about, as well as her devotion to her fans. The combination of these is the embodiment of her desire to provide style at a price her fans can afford. In contrast, Aguilera is also committed to causes that further the betterment of humanity. Clearly there is an ethical conflict here that one wonders if Aguilera is even aware of.

The album has 14 tracks that represent the various sounds of her career from her "Genie" era to *Back to Basics*. This project was particularly meaningful to her, as she said: "The early hits still have a lot of sentimental value for me. Those were the songs that threw me into this whole whirlwind."[6] Also creating quite a sensation was Target's commercial for the album that featured Aguilera as a superhero karate kicking her way through a shortened rendition of the song "Keeps Gettin' Better."

The songs included on the *Keeps Gettin' Better* album include:

"Genie in a Bottle"	3:36
"What a Girl Wants"	3:35
"I Turn to You"	4:39

"Come on over Baby (All I Want Is You)"	3:23
"Dirrty"	4:45
"Fighter"	4:05
"Beautiful"	3:59
"Ain't No Other Man"	3:48
"Candyman"	3:14
"Hurt"	4:03
"Genie 2.0"	4:15
"Keeps Gettin' Better"	3:04
"Dynamite"	3:09
"You Are What You Are (Beautiful)"	4:44

In an innovative and first-ever approach, the video version of the *Keeps Gettin' Better* premier was shown only on iLike, a social network for music and music aficionados. Ali Partovi, CEO of iLike said: "For an artist of her caliber to be the first major artist to debut a new music video on iLike is a milestone for us."[7] Thus is yet another example of Aguilera's tendency to stray off the beaten path of a commercial approach.

BIONIC WOMAN

Released in June 2010, Aguilera has credited the "voice" of her album *Bionic* to her son Max, whom she said is her "musical inspiration who's 'motivating me to play and want to have fun.'"[8] Indeed, the sound of the music on this album is very different from her trademark sound. Still pure Aguilera, the sounds of this LP she has described as softer and more mellow. Ironically, she said, "that maybe I've been afraid to do [this] in the past, to allow myself to go to a place of 'less singing.' I'm more vulnerable and more strong at the same time."[9] Aguilera's first album since 2006 was produced by her pick: Tricky Stewart, who has produced works for Jennifer Lopez, Britney Spears, and Mariah Carey. In fact, Stewart said she's once again mixing sounds: R&B, pop, but it works and is among her best collections of work.

Says writer James Dinh:

Whether she's working with legendary hip-hop producer DJ Premier or making a song that's a throwback to the 1940s, Christina Aguilera has never been afraid to experiment with her music.[10]

DJ QUEEN

In yet another example of her unique and unusual ways of reinventing herself, on August 7, 2009, Aguilera's very own radio station was launched, and this time, instead of singer, she plays the part of disc jockey. The station is hosted on the iheartradio network of Clear Channel Radio, and the format is a combination of news, commentary from Aguilera, interviews, and Aguilera's favorite music. However, the question is, why a radio channel? Aguilera says:

> In the beginning when I make my CDs, I make inspiration record-CDs and I hand them out to all the producers that I am looking forward to working with. And I had out these CDs and at the end of the day it's funny because all the producers or a lot of the producers are like "Wow, you should be a DJ." It's a really great mix of songs and they're so different and eclectic and that's my style in general.[11]

Clear Channel has its origins in 1972 as a small company in San Antonio, Texas, and then went "clear channel," meaning it had its own nationwide frequency, in 1975. Its growth was fueled by the continual purchase of radio stations throughout the country, which then segued into a series of acquisitions and mergers, most recently a $24 billion merger with a subsidiary of CC Media Holdings, Inc. However, in 2009, as a result of the widespread economic downturn, which meant a significant decrease in radio advertising sales, Clear Channel cut its workforce 9 percent by eliminating 1,850 jobs.[12]

Although it was never stated, the motivation for this move was surely additional exposure to Aguilera's fans from a one-stop-shop venue. The music is an eclectic mix of rock, pop, rap, and Aguilera. In addition, the station gives her the opportunity to sell her albums. On 24/7, listeners can tune in online, through their iPhone or BlackBerry.

HUMANITARIAN WORKS
World Hunger Relief

Known for her humanitarian and public service work, Aguilera has also demonstrated concern for those in the world with significantly less. On

Christina Aguilera is photographed backstage at the 67th Annual Golden Globe Awards in Beverly Hills, California, January 17, 2010. AP Photo/Mark J. Terrill.

July 15, 2009, she was named global spokesperson for Yum! Brands and its World Hunger Relief program. Yum! Brands is the largest restaurant company in the world with 36,000 restaurants in 110 countries. Despite a worldwide recession, Yum! Brands still achieved a 20 percent return on investment in 2008 from its four main brands: KFC, Pizza Hut, Taco Bell, and Long John Silver's. It also owns A&W All American restaurants. The driving force behind the company's success is its worldwide penetration with 700 international franchises and more on the way coupled with its reputation for quality. For example, the most successful Kentucky Fried Chicken outlets anywhere in the world are in France. Likewise, in India, Pizza Hut was voted the number one most trusted food service brand. Last, in Russia, a popular fast food company, Rostik's, has teamed up with Kentucky Fried Chicken to form the Rostik's/KFC brand.[13]

In 2009, global hunger rose to epic proportions with more than 1 billion people hungry. The reasons for the sharp increase include global economic issues, higher food costs, severe droughts and floods, and growing food demands in Asia and South America. The goal is to bring awareness of the issues of world hunger to the forefront through public service announcements in which Aguilera will star, as well as posters in all of the brands' restaurants.

However, simply starring in the infomercials was not enough for Aguilera. She and Bratman wanted to see the hunger issue firsthand, so they traveled to Guatemala, in the highlands near Lake Atitlan. They traveled to villages in the area where 60 percent of native children are malnourished.[14] Particularly moving for Aguilera was Concepción, a 25-year-old mother of one with another one on the way whose husband left her and who had no food. When they met, Concepción was standing in a small hut with a dirt floor and a stove for cooking and warmth. Aguilera said:

> I wanted to see with my own eyes what hunger means. As a mom my heart just breaks when I see how young mothers like Concepcion struggle to feed their children. I don't think I can ever forget these images.[15]

One of the things that particularly affected Aguilera was the small size of the children. She said: "One of the biggest lessons I'm taking away from this is the importance of healthy food. If a child under two doesn't get the nutrients they need, we can never fix the damage later on."[16] Children who suffer from malnutrition exhibit some of these symptoms:

- Irritable (bad mood) and tired
- Very slow, or no, growth
- Weight loss
- Bone or joint pain
- Weak muscles
- Bloated abdomen and swelling in other parts of the body
- Brittle, dry skin and hair
- Brittle and spooned nails
- Scaly skin
- Hair loss
- Loss of appetite
- Slow to heal
- Easily get infections
- Sunken temples

Seeing such horrors in young children must have been a terrible shock and heartbreaker to Aguilera and certainly a source of great motivation for her support of the program.

The Yum! Brands program is the largest private sector effort for world hunger and its aims are to raise awareness of the issue, encourage volunteerism, and collect and coordinate funds for the United Nations World Food Programme as well as other charitable agencies and organizations. Whether motivated strictly for publicity or not, Aguilera's involvement in this program is indicative of a young woman who seemingly cares greatly about the world in which she lives.

Way to Go: Vote!

Another example of Aguilera's commitment to make the world a better place is her public service involvements in Rock the Vote, a project to bring awareness of the importance of voting to young people. She was, she said, inspired to get involved because of her son Max. When on the *Larry King Live* show, Aguilera said:

> My involvement with "Rock the Vote" is just trying to bring awareness to everybody out there. In particular for me, being a new mother, you know, it was really important for me to get involved and get excited about this election [2008] in particular, being such one of change and new development for our country and for the future of my son.[17]

Her specific role was to sing "America the Beautiful" on tape, while holding her son Max. Why holding Max?

> But it was really, really nice to bring it down to a really intimate moment between me and my son and kind of symbolizing what this song means in the sense that it's passing it on to the next generation.[18]

In addition, Aguilera admitted that her son would be subjected to media exposure many times and that to have at least one exposure where she was in control was a positive thing.

While growing up, politics was not something discussed in her family, and so Aguilera grew up ignoring the issues of the day. As she grew older, and after processing the domestic abuse she experienced, she came to realize the importance of having a voice, especially for women. Therefore, in addition to her own involvement, she decided it was important to use her celebrity to awaken other young people to the importance of voting.

She was also officially involved in the previous presidential election where she participated in the program Declare Yourself with Norman Lear. Still a viable program, Declare Yourself strives to encourage all 18- to 29-year-old citizens to register and vote in state and national elections. The program is nonpartisan and nonprofit and leverages a myriad of resources to spread the message including retail establishments, celebrities, and mobile technology and the Internet. Declare Yourself has been successful in the sense that it was directly responsible for getting 4 million young people to register to vote.

With an unprecedented turnout for the 2008 elections, Aguilera cites Barak Obama as the catalyst for the change in voter turnout, particularly among youth:

Christina Aguilera poses at the
Esquire House Hollywood Hills
Rock the Vote party in Los Angeles,
September 25, 2008. AP Photo/
Dan Steinberg.

It's exciting, you know? And also, you know, I think, you know, of course, Obama being so huge and everything, he just represents so much—just ground-breaking, history-making, just what an incredible moment, you know.[19]

A BUSY YOUNG WOMAN

Burlesque

Although in public she appears to be extroverted and confident, Aguilera claims to be very shy in real life. In her very first movie role, where she plays the part of a shy young woman, she should be able to tap into her personal experiences to strengthen the authenticity of her character. Aguilera stars in *Burlesque* with Cher, a woman about whom Aguilera said she would "drink her bathwater."[20] Aguilera apparently reveres Cher, despite rumors of some issues between them. Aguilera described working with Cher as a "huge blessing" and added: "I can tell you I love her. I love Cher!"[21] On the other hand, Cher admitted to feeling her age against all her much younger co-stars. "It is a hard job," she said. "You get up at 5AM and you try to look good. All these girls are, like, a third my age. That is rough."[22]

The story line is that of a young and ambitious small town girl from Iowa who leaves home to go to Los Angeles to find success. She becomes employed in a modern-day burlesque club, owned by Cher's character. The relationship between the two characters in the film is close, with Cher giving Aguilera the break she needs to make it big. Interestingly, this film is the first where Cher sings as part of her role. Anticipation for the film among critics is high, with many hinting at its hit potential.[23]

Dancing is a significant part of her role in the film, and so to become a dancing queen for her role in *Burlesque*, Aguilera sought to perfect her skills by taking dancing lessons from Dita Von Teese, who like Aguilera, is fascinated with the retro style of the 1940s. A former stripper, she is known for her burlesque performances and is dubbed "Queen of Burlesque" by the press. Just like with everything she does, Aguilera strove for perfection and insisted on performing her own dance numbers as opposed to allowing doubles to stand in for her.

The film is directed by Steve Antin, brother to *Pussycat Dolls* film creator Robin Antin, and her co-stars, besides Cher, are Kristen Bell

(*Veronica Mars* television show) and Julianne Hough (two-time winner on *Dancing with the Stars*).

Interesting and Offbeat Projects

In a 2009 episode of the television program *Project Runway* (Lifetime), to the thrill of designers who competed with one another to create runway-worthy outfits, Aguilera was their subject. Alongside famous designer Bob Mackie as a judge, the contestants, with just $300 in their pockets, set about the process of designing a masterpiece creation for Aguilera in just two days. None of the results was reportedly impressive, but Aguilera was most gracious and offered kudos for effort if not results.

With her characteristic grace and kindness, Aguilera said to bring-up-the-rear designer Christopher Straub, "You get a big E for effort." The other judges' comments were not as kind.

At the Emmy Award ceremony in 2007, a night honoring Tony Bennett with seven awards for his special *Tony Bennett: An American Classic*, Bennett was ecstatic to perform with Aguilera. The entire experience made him feel "on top of the world again."[24] In addition, it was a celebrity celebration of the joining of eras.

In 2008, Macy's celebrated its 150th anniversary, and Aguilera was a part of the festivities, alongside other modern icons including Martha Stewart, Donald Trump, Tommy Hilfiger, and Calvin Klein. In a true and total celebration of Macy's, these five celebrities were to be photographed by world-famous *Rolling Stone* photographer Mark Seliger, each with one of the most renowned symbols of the overall Macy's brand. Aguilera was photographed to commemorate Macy's Flower Shops; Tommy Hilfiger, Macy's Fourth of July Fireworks; Donald Trump, Macy's Thanksgiving Day Parade; Calvin Klein, Macy's fashion portfolio; and Martha Stewart, Macy's lifestyle and holiday contributions.[25] Macy's has 800 stores in 45 states, the District of Columbia, Puerto Rico, and Guam. For Aguilera to be named a select and strategic player in this celebration is further testimony to her continued growth as not only a star performer, but more important, an influential member of society and culture.

Aguilera's red lips have become a trademark throughout the industry and represent her bold re-entry into the world of 1920s, 1930s, and

Tony Bennett and Christina Aguilera perform the song "Steppin' Out" during the 59th Primetime Emmy Awards in Los Angeles, September 16, 2007. AP Photo/ Mark J. Terrill.

1940s glamour. But red is not limited to her lips, she incorporates the color into every aspect of her wardrobe as well. She said:

> Red is a colour [sic] that defines sexy, whether it's a sultry red lipstick, hot-red-stilettos or a glamorous red evening gown. It's a sensual and feminine color that fuses confidence with classic Hollywood glamour.[26]

Red is indeed filled with symbolism and meaning and is associated with energy, danger, power, passion, desire, and love. It is an intense color, associated with influencing emotions and metabolic functions. From a visibility standpoint, it is effective to use in signals and signs where immediate action is necessary. In graphic and Web design, red is used to make things stand out such as banners, buttons, and images. In advertising, it is the single most erotic color, as in Aguilera's lips.[27]

Besides wearing red "something," Aguilera said there are three regimens by which she swears for her personal beauty regimen. First is facial and body moisturizer, which she said gives her clear, glowing skin. Second is sleep to make every part of the body look good. Finally, she advises hydrating: drinking plenty of water. Such a simple regimen certainly belies her stunning beauty, perfect skin, and ever-present glow.

However, there is one caveat here, and it has to do with her famous red lips. In recent days, she has often been captured in photographs with a shimmering light pink shade, a color that is overtaking the fashion world. Perhaps also the shade leaves a more subtle lip mark on the cheek of her most important young star, son Max.

Aguilera has joined the lineup of the many celebrities now putting their names to fragrance. Some of those include her ever-present competitor Britney Spears, Mariah Carey, Celine Dion, and Paris Hilton. Aguilera now has three fragrances carrying her name. The first namesake was called, simply, "Christina Aguilera" and was introduced in Europe in 2007 but never made it to the United States. Despite its notable bottle in the shape of a women's body covered with lace, the fragrance fell far short of gleaning positive reviews.

Introduced in 2008, "Inspire" was Aguilera's second fragrance namesake and it received a more positive reception. Last is "Christina Aguilera by Night," which was launched in late 2009 with great fanfare and a stunningly sexy promotional video starring Aguilera.

ONWARD AND UPWARD

Her march has been remarkable, but most would say, at least agewise, she's only just begun. Yet even before she reached the age of 30, Aguilera has racked up more awards, distinctions, and accomplishments than most people can dream of. Beginning in childhood, Aguilera learned how to make lemonade from lemons, and bitter ones at that. She channeled her fear and sadness away from the abuse in her family to instead create the music that became her art and her livelihood. Many children, and even adults, become stuck in the mire of their angst, never learning how to use it to get above and beyond. Not so with Aguilera.

Christina Aguilera poses at her "Inspire" fragrance launch at Macy's in New York, September 2, 2008. AP Photo/Evan Agostini.

Starting at a very young age, this young woman exhibited strength of character unusual in most human beings of any age.

What she somehow managed in spite of childhood nightmares, in spite of others trying to control her, in spite of the ups and downs of a cutthroat, and cruelly competitive, business was to cut loose from the forces that could have ruined her, that in fact, tried to use her for their own purposes. Aguilera refused to become a lump of clay to be molded and shaped as anyone wanted. Rather, she chose to channel her life experiences and talents into the kiln of exquisite porcelain: a clay fired at extraordinarily high temperatures to form a beautiful, tough, translucent, and treasured, material.

Somehow, Aguilera gives the world the impression that she has only just begun in every facet of her life, yet she has already accomplished more than most people can even dream of accomplishing. She has won multiple Grammys, is at the top of the heap of recording artists, displays an altruistic commitment to human service, is a devoted mother and wife, and is one of the richest women in show business. Finally:

Aguilera's always been an artist that moves the bar and that's what the great ones do.[28]

NOTES

1. Patrick Barwise and Sean Meehan, "Bullseye: Target's Cheap Chic Strategy," *Harvard Business School: Working Knowledge for Business Leaders*, retrieved January 13, 2010, from http://hbswk.hbs.edu/archive/4319.html.

2. Mya Frazier, "The Latest European Import: Fast Fashion," *Advertising Age*, January 9, 2006.

3. Ibid.

4. Suzy Menkes, "Is Fast Fashion Going out of Fashion?" New York Times.com, September 21, 2008, retrieved March 16, 2010, from http://www.nytimes.com/2008/09/21/style/21iht-rbasta.1.16332117.html?pagewanted=1&_r=1.

5. Ibid.

6. Adrian Thrills, "Britney? I Wish Her All the Best . . . Honest!" *Daily Mail* (London), November 7, 2008, LexisNexis para 30.

7. "Christina Aguilera to World-Debut Her New Music Video (*Keeps Gettin' Better*) Exclusively via iLike," Business Wire.com, October 27, 2008, retrieved December 20, 2009, from http://www.ilike.com/artist/Christina+Aguilera.

8. James Dinh, "Singer Takes Electronic Approach with a Slew of Collaborations on New LP," MTV.com, January 5, 2010, retrieved January 7, 2010, from http://www.mtv.com/news/articles/1629061/20100105/aguilera_Aguilera.jhtml.

9. Ibid.

10. James Dinh, "Christina Aguilera Says New Album *Bionic* 'Is about the Future,'" MTV.com, January 5, 2010, retrieved January 7, 2010, from http://www.mtv.com/news/articles/1629061/20100105/aguilera_Aguilera.jhtml.

11. Fekadu, Mesfin, "Christina Aguilera Becomes DJ, Talks Music, Film," ABCNEWS Entertainment, July 30, 2009, retrieved June 29, 2010, from http://abcnews.go.com/Entertainment/wireStory?id=8211393.

12. Deborah Yao, "Clear Channel Cuts 9% of Workforce, Eliminates 1850 Jobs," Huffington Post.com, January 20, 2009, retrieved

March 16, 2010, from http://www.huffingtonpost.com/2009/01/20/clear-channel-cuts-9-of-w_n_159547.html.

13. Yum!, http://www.yum.com.

14. "Christina Aguilera Sees Hunger First Hand in Guatemala," World Food Programme.org, September 23, 2009 retrieved September 24, 2009, from http://www.wfp.org/stories/Aguilera-aguilera-sees-hunger-first-hand-guatemala.

15. Ibid.

16. Ibid.

17. "Predicting the Youth Vote in 2008; Christina Aguilera Rocks the Vote . . ." CNN *Larry King Live*, June 25, 2008.

18. Ibid.

19. Ibid.

20. Gaby Wood, "Queen Aguilera," Marie Claire.com, February 2010, retrieved January 23, 2010, from http://www.marieclaire.com/celebrity-lifestyle/celebrities/interviews/Aguilera-aguilera-interview-2010.

21. Catriona Wightman, "Cher: 'Burlesque Stars Make Me Feel Old,'" Digital Spy.com, February 10, 2010, retrieved March 17, 2010, from http://www.digitalspy.com/movies/news/a201693/cher-burlesque-stars-make-me-feel-old.html.

22. Ibid.

23. Elisabeth Rapp, "Cher Joins Christina Aguilera in 'Burlesque,'" MTV Movies Blog, June 23, 2009, retrieved March 17, 2010, from http://moviesblog.mtv.com/2009/06/23/cher-joins-christina-aguilera-in-burlesque/.

24. "What Becomes a Legend Most," New Zealand Press Association, E-news wire press release, October 10, 2007.

25. "Mark Seliger Captures Macy's 'Stars' for Commemorative 150th Birthday Images," Business Write, July 31, 2008, press release issued by Macy's.

26. "Aguilera Obsessed with Red," IrelandOn-Line, September 23, 2009 retrieved October 4, 2009, from http://breakingnews.iol.ie/entertainment/aguilera-obsessed-with-red-427407.html.

27. "Color Meaning: Red," ColorWheelPro.com, retrieved March 17, 2010, from http://www.color-wheel-pro.com/color-meaning.html.

28. "Christina Aguilera's New Album is D.O.N.E.," New York Post.com, October 1, 2009, retrieved October 17, 2009, from http://www.nypost.com/p/blogs/popwrap/item_2APDHrYbuuQrd0jknbc4dN.

Appendix

AWARDS

RECORDING INDUSTRY ASSOCIATION OF AMERICA (RIAA) SALES AWARDS

Gold Awards (500,000 copies)

- 1999: *Christina Aguilera* (album)
- 1999: "Genie in a Bottle" (single)
- 1999: "What a Girl Wants" (single)
- 2000: "Come on over Baby (All I Want Is You)" (single)
- 2000: *Mi Reflejo* (album)
- 2000: *My Kind of Christmas* (album)
- 2002: *Stripped* (album)
- 2006: "Beautiful" (single)
- 2006: "Fighter" (single)
- 2006: *Back to Basics* (album)
- 2006: "Ain't No Other Man" (single)
- 2007: "Hurt" (single)
- 2007: "Candyman" (single)

Platinum Awards (1 million copies)

- 1999: *Christina Aguilera* (album)
- 1999: "Genie in a Bottle" (single)
- 2000: *Mi Reflejo* (album)
- 2000: *My Kind of Christmas* (album)
- 2002: *Stripped* (album)
- 2006: *Back to Basics* (album)
- 2007: "Ain't No Other Man" (single)

Multi-Platinum Awards (2 million or more)

- 2000: *Christina Aguilera* (album) 8x Platinum (8 million)
- 2001: *Mi Reflejo* (album) 6x Platinum (6 million)
- 2005: *Stripped* (album) 4x Platinum (4 million)

Amigo Award

- Best International Newcomer (2000)
- Best International Female Artist (2003)
- Best International Album (2003)
- Best International Album (2006)

ALMA AWARDS

Year	Nominated Work	Award	Result
1999	"Reflection"	Outstanding Performance of a Song for a Feature Film	Nominated
2000	Christina Aguilera	New Entertainer of the Year	Won
2002	43rd Grammy Awards	Outstanding Performance in a Music, Variety or Comedy Special	Nominated
	"Lady Marmalade"	Outstanding Song in a Motion Picture Soundtrack	Won
2009	Christina Aguilera	Best of the Year in Music	Nominated

ASCAP POP MUSIC AWARDS

- "Come on over Baby (All I Want Is You)" (2002)
- "Lady Marmalade" (2002)
- "Miss Independent" (Kelly Clarkson) (2003)
- "Beautiful" (2004)
- "Can't Hold Us Down" (2005)
- "Ain't No Other Man" (2008)
- "Hurt" (2008)
- "Candyman" (2008)

BILLBOARD LATIN MUSIC AWARDS

Year	Nominated Work	Award	Result
2001	Mi Reflejo	Pop Album of the Year, Female	Won
		Pop Album of the Year, New Artist	Won

BILLBOARD MUSIC AWARD

Year	Nominated Work	Award	Result
2000	Christina Aguilera	Female Artist of the Year	Won

BILLBOARD TOURING AWARDS

Year	Nominated Work	Award	Result
2007	Back to Basics Tour	Top Package	Nominated
		Breakthrough Artist	Nominated

BILLBOARD VIDEO AWARD

- Director of the Year (Paul Hunter): "Lady Marmalade" (2002)

BLOCKBUSTER ENTERTAINMENT AWARDS

Year	Nominated Work	Award	Result
2000	"Genie in a Bottle"	Favorite New Female Artist	Won
		Favorite Single	Won
2001	Christina Aguilera	Favorite Female Artist of the Year	Won
	Mi Reflejo	Favorite Latin Album of the Year	Won

BMI AWARDS

Year	Nominated Work	Award	Result
2000	"Genie in a Bottle"		Won
2001	"What a Girl Wants"		Won
2002	"Come on over Baby (All I Want Is You)"		Won
	"Lady Marmalade"		Won
2004	"Miss Independent" (Kelly Clarkson)		Won
2008	"Ain't No Other Man"		Won
	"Hurt"		Won

BRIT AWARDS

Year	Nominated Work	Award	Result
2004	Christina Aguilera	International Female Solo Artist	Nominated
		Pop Act	Nominated
	Stripped	International Album	Nominated
2007	Christina Aguilera	International Female Solo Artist	Nominated

ENTERTAINMENT NEWS AWARD

- Best Dressed at Grammys (2001)

ENTERTAINMENT WEEKLY AWARD

- "Must-List" Entertainer of the Year (2006)

GLAMOUR WOMEN OF THE YEAR AWARD

- Woman of the Year (2004)

GOLDEN GLOBE AWARD

- "Reflection": Best Original Song—Nominated (1998)

GRAMMY AWARDS

Year	Nominated Work	Award	Result
2000	Christina Aguilera	Best New Artist	Won
	"Genie in a Bottle"	Best Female Pop Vocal Performance	Nominated
2001	"What a Girl Wants"	Best Female Pop Vocal Performance	Nominated
	Mi Reflejo	Best Latin Pop Album	Nominated
2002	"Nobody Wants to Be Lonely" (with Ricky Martin)	Best Pop Collaboration with Vocals	Nominated
	"Lady Marmalade" (with Lil' Kim, Mýa, and Pink)	Best Pop Collaboration with Vocals	Won
2003	"Dirrty" (featuring Redman)	Best Pop Collaboration with Vocals	Nominated
2004	"Can't Hold Us Down" (featuring Lil' Kim)	Best Pop Collaboration with Vocals	Nominated
	Stripped	Best Pop Vocal Album	Nominated
	"Beautiful"	Best Female Pop Vocal Performance	Won
2006	"A Song for You" (with Herbie Hancock)	Best Pop Collaboration with Vocals	Nominated
2007	"Ain't No Other Man"	Best Female Pop Vocal Performance	Won
	Back to Basics	Best Pop Vocal Album	Nominated
2008	"Candyman"	Best Female Pop Vocal Performance	Nominated
	"Steppin' Out" (with Tony Bennett)	Best Pop Collaboration with Vocals	Nominated

LATIN GRAMMY AWARDS

Year	Nominated Work	Award	Result
2000	"Genio Atrapado"	Best Female Pop Vocal Performance	Nominated
2001	"Pero Me Acuerdo de Ti"	Record of the Year	Nominated
	Mi Reflejo	Best Female Pop Vocal Album	Won

INTERNATIONAL DANCE MUSIC AWARDS

Year	Nominated Work	Award	Result
2007	"Ain't No Other Man"	Best Pop Dance Track	Nominated
		Best Dance Music Video	Nominated

ITUNES AWARD

Year	Nominated Work	Award	Result
2006	Back to Basics	Best Pop Album of the Year	Won

IVOR NOVELLO AWARD

Year	Nominated Work	Award	Result
1999	"Genie in a Bottle"	International Hit of the Year	Won

JUNO AWARDS

Year	Nominated Work	Award	Result
2004	*Stripped*	International Album of the Year	Nominated
	"Fighter"	Video of the Year	Won
2007	"Hurt"	Video of the Year	Nominated

LADIES' HOME JOURNAL

- Top 10 Most Fascinating Women of 1999 (1999)

LATINA MAGAZINE

- Entertainer of the Year (2000)
- Women of the Year (2003)

MAXIM MAGAZINE

- Woman of the Year: Best International Female Singer (2000)
- Sexiest Woman of the Year (2003)
- Most Awesome Video: "Ain't No Other Man" (2006)

MTV VIDEO MUSIC AWARDS

Year	Nominated Work	Award	Result
2000	"What a Girl Wants"	Best Female Video	Nominated
		Best Pop Video	Nominated
		Best New Artist	Nominated
		Viewer's Choice	Nominated
		Best Choreography	Nominated

(Continued)

Year	Nominated Work	Award	Result
2001	"Lady Marmalade" (with Lil' Kim, Mýa, and Pink)	Video of the Year	Won
		Best Video from a Film	Won
		Best Pop Video	Nominated
		Best Dance Video	Nominated
		Best Choreography	Nominated
		Best Art Direction	Nominated
2003	"Dirrty" (featuring Redman)	Best Female Video	Nominated
		Best Dance Video	Nominated
		Best Pop Video	Nominated
		Best Choreography	Nominated
2004	"The Voice Within"	Best Female Video	Nominated
		Viewer's Choice	Nominated
		Best Cinematography	Nominated
2006	"Ain't No Other Man"	Video of the Year	Nominated
		Best Female Video	Nominated
		Best Pop Video	Nominated
		Best Choreography	Nominated
2007	"Candyman"	Best Director	Nominated
2000	"Genie in a Bottle"	People's Choice: Favorite International Artist	Nominated
2004	"The Voice Within"	Best International Artist Video	Nominated
2007	"Candyman"	Best International Artist Video	Nominated

MVPA VIDEO AWARDS

- Best R&B Video: "What's Going On"—Artists against AIDS (2002)
- Best Styling in a Video: "Lady Marmalade" (2002)
- Best Styling in a Video: "Dirrty" (2002)
- Best Make-Up: "Dirrty" (2002)
- Best Pop Video: "Fighter" (Floria Sigismondi) (2004)
- Most Fashionable Music Video: "Can't Hold Us Down" (2004)

- Best Cinematography: "Fighter" (2004)
- Best Make-Up: "Fighter" (2004)
- Best Styling in a Video: "Fighter" (2004)
- Video of the Year: "Hurt" (Floria Sigismondi and Christina Aguilera) (2007)
- Best Art Direction: "Candyman" (Matthew Rolston and Christina Aguilera) (2009)

OVMA

- Female Artist of the Year (2002)
- Best Female Video: "Dirrty" (2002)
- Best U.S.A. Artist (2002)
- Female Artist of the Year (2003)
- Best Female Video: "Fighter" (2003)
- Best Pop Vocal Performance: "Beautiful" (2003)
- Best Pop Video: "Fighter" (2003)
- Best Comeback (2003)
- Artist of the Year (2003)
- Best U.S.A. Artist (2003)
- Female Artist of the Year (2004)
- Best Female Video: "The Voice Within" (2004)
- Best Pop Vocal Performance in a Video: "The Voice Within" (2004)
- Video of the Year: "The Voice Within" (2004)
- Album of the Year: *Stripped* (2004)
- Best Pop Vocal Performance in a Video: "Tilt Ya Head Back" feat. (2005)
- Female Artist of the Year (2006)
- Album of the Year: *Back to Basics* (2006)
- Best Female Video: "Ain't No Other Man" (2006)
- Best Pop Video: "Hurt" (2007)
- Best Editing: "Candyman" (2007)
- Best Costume in a Video (Female): "Hurt" (2007)
- Best Female Video: "Hurt" (2007)
- Video of the Year: "Hurt" (2007)

PEOPLE'S CHOICE AWARDS

Year	Nominated Work	Award	Result
2005	"Car Wash" (with Missy Elliott)	Favorite Remake	Nominated
		Favorite Combined Forces	Nominated
2007	"Ain't No Other Man"	Favorite R&B Song	Nominated

ROLLING STONE MAGAZINE

- Best Female Performer, Readers' Pick (2003)
- Best Tour, Readers' Pick: *Justified* and *Stripped* Tour (2003)
- Best Female Performer, Readers' Pick (2006)
- Best R&B Artist, Readers' Pick (2006)

TEEN.COM AWARD

- Best CD: *Christina Aguilera* (1999)
- Best Female Artist (1999)
- Best Song Female Artist: "Genie in a Bottle" (1999)
- Best Female Artist (2003)
- Best Song Female Artist: "Beautiful" (2003)
- Best Female Artist (2006)
- Best Sad Song Female Artist: "Hurt" (2006)
- Best CD: *Back to Basics* (2006)

FURTHER READING

BOOK

Dominguez, Pier. *Christina Aguilera: A Star Is Made*. Phoenix: Colossus Books, 2003.

ARTICLES: CHRISTINA AGUILERA

Bozza, Anthony. "The Christina Aguilera Story (so far)." *Rolling Stone,* October 28, 1999.

"Christina Aguilera Marries." People.com, November 21, 2005. Retrieved January 6, 2010, from http://www.people.com/people/article/0,,1131176,00.html?cid=redirect-articles/.

"Christina Aguilera Says Becoming a Mom Has Stopped Her from Being Loud and Impatient." *Daily News* (New York), March 15, 2009.

Harrington, Richard. "Christina Aguilera's Fast Track: Ex-Mouseketeer Has the Voice to Pull Away from Teen Pop Pack." *Washington Post,* February 13, 2000.

Holden, Moira. "Christina Talks about Dad's 'Abuse.'" UKfamily.co.uk, September 2009, http://ukfamily.co.uk/lifestyle/news/2009–9/general/christina-aguilera-dad-abuse.html.

Masley, Ed. "Blessed by a 'Genie.'" *Pittsburgh Post Gazette*, August 13, 1999.

Pulvirenti, Angela. "It Hurts So Much—I'm Not That Kind of Girl." *Sunday Telegraph Magazine* (Sydney, Australia), June 8, 2003.

Sandell, Laurie. "Christina: Intimate Talk about a Past That Still Hurts." Glamour.com, December 1, 2006. Retrieved August 4, 2009 from http://www.glamour.com/magazine/2006/12/christina-aguilera.

Sandell, Laurie. "Christina (without all the drama)." Glamour.com, July 1, 2008. Retrieved June 23, 2009 from http://www.glamour.com/magazine/2008/07/christina-aguilera.

Sheffield, Rob. "Christina Aguilera's Bottle Rocket." *Rolling Stone*, August 19, 1999. Retrieved July 23, 2009.

ARTICLES: BACKGROUND AND SUPPORT MATERIAL

"Disneyland's History." Just Disney.com, http://www.justdisney.com/disney land/history.html.

Galenson, David. "From 'White Christmas' to Sgt. Pepper: The Conceptual Revolution in Popular Music." *Historical Methods* 42, no. 1 (Winter 2009): 19.

"Hispanic Heritage: Christina Aguilera." Gale Cengage Learning. Retrieved September 1, 2009 from http://www.gale.cengage.com/free_resources/chh/bio/aguilera_c.htm.

"Jordan Bratman Bio." Yuddy.com. Retrieved January 13, 2010 from http://www.yuddy.com/celebrity/jordan-bratman/bio.

"Walt Disney's Disneyland." Just Disney.com. Retrieved August 1, 2009 from http://www.justdisney.com/walt_disney/biography/w_disneyland.html.

"What Becomes a Legend Most." New Zealand Press Association, October 10, 2007.

WEB SITES

Christina Aguilera Official Web Site: www.christinaaguilera.com/

Christina Aguilera Perfumes: http://www.christina-aguilera-perfumes.com/

Christina Aguilera's Site: http://www.simplyaguilera.com/

INDEX

About the Author

MARY ANNE DONOVAN is the author of numerous articles and several books, including *How to Train the Harness Racehorse* and *How I Hate to Date Online*. She has also developed content for a myriad of Web sites as well as served as editor for *Writer Online*, a writers' Web site once recognized as the number one Web site for writers by *Writer's Digest* magazine. She holds a master's degree and is an adjunct writing professor for both the State University of New York at Brockport and Colorado Technical University.

www.ingramcontent.com/pod-product-compliance
Lightning Source LLC
Chambersburg PA
CBHW070443100426
42812CB00004B/1191